Mometrix
TEST PREPARATION

ITBS
Success Strategies
Level 10 Grade 4

D1567154

DEAR FUTURE EXAM SUCCESS STORY

First of all, **THANK YOU** for purchasing Mometrix study materials!

Second, congratulations! You are one of the few determined test-takers who are committed to doing whatever it takes to excel on your exam. **You have come to the right place.** We developed these study materials with one goal in mind: to deliver you the information you need in a format that's concise and easy to use.

In addition to optimizing your guide for the content of the test, we've outlined our recommended steps for breaking down the preparation process into small, attainable goals so you can make sure you stay on track.

We've also analyzed the entire test-taking process, identifying the most common pitfalls and showing how you can overcome them and be ready for any curveball the test throws you.

Standardized testing is one of the biggest obstacles on your road to success, which only increases the importance of doing well in the high-pressure, high-stakes environment of test day. Your results on this test could have a significant impact on your future, and this guide provides the information and practical advice to help you achieve your full potential on test day.

Your success is our success

We would love to hear from you! If you would like to share the story of your exam success or if you have any questions or comments in regard to our products, please contact us at **800-673-8175** or **support@mometrix.com**.

Thanks again for your business and we wish you continued success!

Sincerely,
The Mometrix Test Preparation Team

TABLE OF CONTENTS

Introduction

Thank you for purchasing this resource! You have made the choice to prepare yourself for a test that could have a huge impact on your future, and this guide is designed to help you be fully ready for test day. Obviously, it's important to have a solid understanding of the test material, but you also need to be prepared for the unique environment and stressors of the test, so that you can perform to the best of your abilities.

For this purpose, the first section that appears in this guide is the **Success Strategies**. We've devoted countless hours to meticulously researching what works and what doesn't, and we've boiled down our findings to the five most impactful steps you can take to improve your performance on the test. We start at the beginning with study planning and move through the preparation process, all the way to the testing strategies that will help you get the most out of what you know when you're finally sitting in front of the test.

We recommend that you start preparing for your test as far in advance as possible. However, if you've bought this guide as a last-minute study resource and only have a few days before your test, we recommend that you skip over the first two Success Strategies since they address a long-term study plan.

If you struggle with **test anxiety**, we strongly encourage you to check out our recommendations for how you can overcome it. Test anxiety is a formidable foe, but it can be beaten, and we want to make sure you have the tools you need to defeat it.

1

Strategy #1 – Plan Big, Study Small

There's a lot riding on your performance. If you want to ace this test, you're going to need to keep your skills sharp and the material fresh in your mind. You need a plan that lets you review everything you need to know while still fitting in your schedule. We'll break this strategy down into three categories.

Information Organization

Start with the information you already have: the official test outline. From this, you can make a complete list of all the concepts you need to cover before the test. Organize these concepts into groups that can be studied together, and create a list of any related vocabulary you need to learn so you can brush up on any difficult terms. You'll want to keep this vocabulary list handy once you actually start studying since you may need to add to it along the way.

Time Management

Once you have your set of study concepts, decide how to spread them out over the time you have left before the test. Break your study plan into small, clear goals so you have a manageable task for each day and know exactly what you're doing. Then just focus on one small step at a time. When you manage your time this way, you don't need to spend hours at a time studying. Studying a small block of content for a short period each day helps you retain information better and avoid stressing over how much you have left to do. You can relax knowing that you have a plan to cover everything in time. In order for this strategy to be effective though, you have to start studying early and stick to your schedule. Avoid the exhaustion and futility that comes from last-minute cramming!

Study Environment

The environment you study in has a big impact on your learning. Studying in a coffee shop, while probably more enjoyable, is not likely to be as fruitful as studying in a quiet room. It's important to keep distractions to a minimum. You're only planning to study for a short block of time, so make the most of it. Don't pause to check your phone or get up to find a snack. It's also important to **avoid multitasking**. Research has consistently shown that multitasking will make your studying dramatically less effective. Your study area should also be comfortable and well-lit so you don't have the distraction of straining your eyes or sitting on an uncomfortable chair.

 The time of day you study is also important. You want to be rested and alert. Don't wait until just before bedtime. Study when you'll be most likely to comprehend and remember. Even better, if you know what time of day your test will be, set that time aside for study. That way your brain will be used to working on that subject at that specific time and you'll have a better chance of recalling information.

Finally, it can be helpful to team up with others who are studying for the same test. Your actual studying should be done in as isolated an environment as possible, but the work of organizing the information and setting up the study plan can be divided up. In between study sessions, you can discuss with your teammates the concepts that you're all studying and quiz each other on the details. Just be sure that your teammates are as serious about the test as you are. If you find that your study time is being replaced with social time, you might need to find a new team.

Strategy #2 – Make Your Studying Count

You're devoting a lot of time and effort to preparing for this test, so you want to be absolutely certain it will pay off. This means doing more than just reading the content and hoping you can remember it on test day. It's important to make every minute of study count. There are two main areas you can focus on to make your studying count.

Retention

It doesn't matter how much time you study if you can't remember the material. You need to make sure you are retaining the concepts. To check your retention of the information you're learning, try recalling it at later times with minimal prompting. Try carrying around flashcards and glance at one or two from time to time or ask a friend who's also studying for the test to quiz you.

To enhance your retention, look for ways to put the information into practice so that you can apply it rather than simply recalling it. If you're using the information in practical ways, it will be much easier to remember. Similarly, it helps to solidify a concept in your mind if you're not only reading it to yourself but also explaining it to someone else. Ask a friend to let you teach them about a concept you're a little shaky on (or speak aloud to an imaginary audience if necessary). As you try to summarize, define, give examples, and answer your friend's questions, you'll understand the concepts better and they will stay with you longer. Finally, step back for a big picture view and ask yourself how each piece of information fits with the whole subject. When you link the different concepts together and see them working together as a whole, it's easier to remember the individual components.

Finally, practice showing your work on any multi-step problems, even if you're just studying. Writing out each step you take to solve a problem will help solidify the process in your mind, and you'll be more likely to remember it during the test.

Modality

Modality simply refers to the means or method by which you study. Choosing a study modality that fits your own individual learning style is crucial. No two people learn best in exactly the same way, so it's important to know your strengths and use them to your advantage.

For example, if you learn best by visualization, focus on visualizing a concept in your mind and draw an image or a diagram. Try color-coding your notes, illustrating them, or creating symbols that will trigger your mind to recall a learned concept. If you learn best by hearing or discussing information, find a study partner who learns the same way or read aloud to yourself. Think about how to put the information in your own words. Imagine that you are giving a lecture on the topic and record yourself so you can listen to it later.

For any learning style, flashcards can be helpful. Organize the information so you can take advantage of spare moments to review. Underline key words or phrases. Use different colors for different categories. Mnemonic devices (such as creating a short list in which every item starts with the same letter) can also help with retention. Find what works best for you and use it to store the information in your mind most effectively and easily.

3

Strategy #3 – Practice the Right Way

Your success on test day depends not only on how many hours you put into preparing, but also on whether you prepared the right way. It's good to check along the way to see if your studying is paying off. One of the most effective ways to do this is by taking practice tests to evaluate your progress. Practice tests are useful because they show exactly where you need to improve. Every time you take a practice test, pay special attention to these three groups of questions:

- The questions you got wrong
- The questions you had to guess on, even if you guessed right
- The questions you found difficult or slow to work through

This will show you exactly what your weak areas are, and where you need to devote more study time. Ask yourself why each of these questions gave you trouble. Was it because you didn't understand the material? Was it because you didn't remember the vocabulary? Do you need more repetitions on this type of question to build speed and confidence? Dig into those questions and figure out how you can strengthen your weak areas as you go back to review the material.

 Additionally, many practice tests have a section explaining the answer choices. It can be tempting to read the explanation and think that you now have a good understanding of the concept. However, an explanation likely only covers part of the question's broader context. Even if the explanation makes perfect sense, **go back and investigate** every concept related to the question until you're positive you have a thorough understanding.

As you go along, keep in mind that the practice test is just that: practice. Memorizing these questions and answers will not be very helpful on the actual test because it is unlikely to have any of the same exact questions. If you only know the right answers to the sample questions, you won't be prepared for the real thing. **Study the concepts** until you understand them fully, and then you'll be able to answer any question that shows up on the test.

It's important to wait on the practice tests until you're ready. If you take a test on your first day of study, you may be overwhelmed by the amount of material covered and how much you need to learn. Work up to it gradually.

On test day, you'll need to be prepared for answering questions, managing your time, and using the test-taking strategies you've learned. It's a lot to balance, like a mental marathon that will have a big impact on your future. Like training for a marathon, you'll need to start slowly and work your way up. When test day arrives, you'll be ready.

Start with the strategies you've read in the first two Success Strategies—plan your course and study in the way that works best for you. If you have time, consider using multiple study resources to get different approaches to the same concepts. It can be helpful to see difficult concepts from more than one angle. Then find a good source for practice tests. Many times, the test website will suggest potential study resources or provide sample tests.

Practice Test Strategy

If you're able to find at least three practice tests, we recommend this strategy:

UNTIMED AND OPEN-BOOK PRACTICE

Take the first test with no time constraints and with your notes and study guide handy. Take your time and focus on applying the strategies you've learned.

TIMED AND OPEN-BOOK PRACTICE

Take the second practice test open-book as well, but set a timer and practice pacing yourself to finish in time.

TIMED AND CLOSED-BOOK PRACTICE

Take any other practice tests as if it were test day. Set a timer and put away your study materials. Sit at a table or desk in a quiet room, imagine yourself at the testing center, and answer questions as quickly and accurately as possible.

Keep repeating timed and closed-book tests on a regular basis until you run out of practice tests or it's time for the actual test. Your mind will be ready for the schedule and stress of test day, and you'll be able to focus on recalling the material you've learned.

Strategy #4 – Pace Yourself

Once you're fully prepared for the material on the test, your biggest challenge on test day will be managing your time. Just knowing that the clock is ticking can make you panic even if you have plenty of time left. Work on pacing yourself so you can build confidence against the time constraints of the exam. Pacing is a difficult skill to master, especially in a high-pressure environment, so **practice is vital**.

Set time expectations for your pace based on how much time is available. For example, if a section has 60 questions and the time limit is 30 minutes, you know you have to average 30 seconds or less per question in order to answer them all. Although 30 seconds is the hard limit, set 25 seconds per question as your goal, so you reserve extra time to spend on harder questions. When you budget extra time for the harder questions, you no longer have any reason to stress when those questions take longer to answer.

Don't let this time expectation distract you from working through the test at a calm, steady pace, but keep it in mind so you don't spend too much time on any one question. Recognize that taking extra time on one question you don't understand may keep you from answering two that you do understand later in the test. If your time limit for a question is up and you're still not sure of the answer, mark it and move on, and come back to it later if the time and the test format allow. If the testing format doesn't allow you to return to earlier questions, just make an educated guess; then put it out of your mind and move on.

On the easier questions, be careful not to rush. It may seem wise to hurry through them so you have more time for the challenging ones, but it's not worth missing one if you know the concept and just didn't take the time to read the question fully. Work efficiently but make sure you understand the question and have looked at all of the answer choices, since more than one may seem right at first.

Even if you're paying attention to the time, you may find yourself a little behind at some point. You should speed up to get back on track, but do so wisely. Don't panic; just take a few seconds less on each question until you're caught up. Don't guess without thinking, but do look through the answer choices and eliminate any you know are wrong. If you can get down to two choices, it is often worthwhile to guess from those. Once you've chosen an answer, move on and don't dwell on any that you skipped or had to hurry through. If a question was taking too long, chances are it was one of the harder ones, so you weren't as likely to get it right anyway.

On the other hand, if you find yourself getting ahead of schedule, it may be beneficial to slow down a little. The more quickly you work, the more likely you are to make a careless mistake that will affect your score. You've budgeted time for each question, so don't be afraid to spend that time. Practice an efficient but careful pace to get the most out of the time you have.

Test-Taking Strategies

This section contains a list of test-taking strategies that you may find helpful as you work through the test. By taking what you know and applying logical thought, you can maximize your chances of answering any question correctly!

It is very important to realize that every question is different and every person is different: no single strategy will work on every question, and no single strategy will work for every person. That's why we've included all of them here, so you can try them out and determine which ones work best for different types of questions and which ones work best for you.

Question Strategies

☑ READ CAREFULLY

Read the question and the answer choices carefully. Don't miss the question because you misread the terms. You have plenty of time to read each question thoroughly and make sure you understand what is being asked. Yet a happy medium must be attained, so don't waste too much time. You must read carefully and efficiently.

☑ CONTEXTUAL CLUES

Look for contextual clues. If the question includes a word you are not familiar with, look at the immediate context for some indication of what the word might mean. Contextual clues can often give you all the information you need to decipher the meaning of an unfamiliar word. Even if you can't determine the meaning, you may be able to narrow down the possibilities enough to make a solid guess at the answer to the question.

☑ PREFIXES

If you're having trouble with a word in the question or answer choices, try dissecting it. Take advantage of every clue that the word might include. Prefixes can be a huge help. Usually, they allow you to determine a basic meaning. *Pre-* means before, *post-* means after, *pro-* is positive, *de-* is negative. From prefixes, you can get an idea of the general meaning of the word and try to put it into context.

☑ HEDGE WORDS

Watch out for critical hedge words, such as *likely, may, can, sometimes, often, almost, mostly, usually, generally, rarely,* and *sometimes.* Question writers insert these hedge phrases to cover every possibility. Often an answer choice will be wrong simply because it leaves no room for exception. Be on guard for answer choices that have definitive words such as *exactly* and *always*.

☑ SWITCHBACK WORDS

Stay alert for *switchbacks*. These are the words and phrases frequently used to alert you to shifts in thought. The most common switchback words are *but, although,* and *however*. Others include *nevertheless, on the other hand, even though, while, in spite of, despite,* and *regardless of.* Switchback words are important to catch because they can change the direction of the question or an answer choice.

7

⊘ FACE VALUE

When in doubt, use common sense. Accept the situation in the problem at face value. Don't read too much into it. These problems will not require you to make wild assumptions. If you have to go beyond creativity and warp time or space in order to have an answer choice fit the question, then you should move on and consider the other answer choices. These are normal problems rooted in reality. The applicable relationship or explanation may not be readily apparent, but it is there for you to figure out. Use your common sense to interpret anything that isn't clear.

Answer Choice Strategies

⊘ ANSWER SELECTION

The most thorough way to pick an answer choice is to identify and eliminate wrong answers until only one is left, then confirm it is the correct answer. Sometimes an answer choice may immediately seem right, but be careful. The test writers will usually put more than one reasonable answer choice on each question, so take a second to read all of them and make sure that the other choices are not equally obvious. As long as you have time left, it is better to read every answer choice than to pick the first one that looks right without checking the others.

⊘ ANSWER CHOICE FAMILIES

An answer choice family consists of two (in rare cases, three) answer choices that are very similar in construction and cannot all be true at the same time. If you see two answer choices that are direct opposites or parallels, one of them is usually the correct answer. For instance, if one answer choice says that quantity x increases and another either says that quantity x decreases (opposite) or says that quantity y increases (parallel), then those answer choices would fall into the same family. An answer choice that doesn't match the construction of the answer choice family is more likely to be incorrect. Most questions will not have answer choice families, but when they do appear, you should be prepared to recognize them.

⊘ ELIMINATE ANSWERS

Eliminate answer choices as soon as you realize they are wrong, but make sure you consider all possibilities. If you are eliminating answer choices and realize that the last one you are left with is also wrong, don't panic. Start over and consider each choice again. There may be something you missed the first time that you will realize on the second pass.

⊘ AVOID FACT TRAPS

Don't be distracted by an answer choice that is factually true but doesn't answer the question. You are looking for the choice that answers the question. Stay focused on what the question is asking for so you don't accidentally pick an answer that is true but incorrect. Always go back to the question and make sure the answer choice you've selected actually answers the question and is not merely a true statement.

⊘ EXTREME STATEMENTS

In general, you should avoid answers that put forth extreme actions as standard practice or proclaim controversial ideas as established fact. An answer choice that states the "process should be used in certain situations, if..." is much more likely to be correct than one that states the "process should be discontinued completely." The first is a calm rational statement and doesn't even make a definitive, uncompromising stance, using a hedge word *if* to provide wiggle room, whereas the second choice is far more extreme.

⌀ BENCHMARK

As you read through the answer choices and you come across one that seems to answer the question well, mentally select that answer choice. This is not your final answer, but it's the one that will help you evaluate the other answer choices. The one that you selected is your benchmark or standard for judging each of the other answer choices. Every other answer choice must be compared to your benchmark. That choice is correct until proven otherwise by another answer choice beating it. If you find a better answer, then that one becomes your new benchmark. Once you've decided that no other choice answers the question as well as your benchmark, you have your final answer.

⌀ PREDICT THE ANSWER

Before you even start looking at the answer choices, it is often best to try to predict the answer. When you come up with the answer on your own, it is easier to avoid distractions and traps because you will know exactly what to look for. The right answer choice is unlikely to be word-for-word what you came up with, but it should be a close match. Even if you are confident that you have the right answer, you should still take the time to read each option before moving on.

General Strategies

⌀ TOUGH QUESTIONS

If you are stumped on a problem or it appears too hard or too difficult, don't waste time. Move on! Remember though, if you can quickly check for obviously incorrect answer choices, your chances of guessing correctly are greatly improved. Before you completely give up, at least try to knock out a couple of possible answers. Eliminate what you can and then guess at the remaining answer choices before moving on.

⌀ CHECK YOUR WORK

Since you will probably not know every term listed and the answer to every question, it is important that you get credit for the ones that you do know. Don't miss any questions through careless mistakes. If at all possible, try to take a second to look back over your answer selection and make sure you've selected the correct answer choice and haven't made a costly careless mistake (such as marking an answer choice that you didn't mean to mark). This quick double check should more than pay for itself in caught mistakes for the time it costs.

⌀ PACE YOURSELF

It's easy to be overwhelmed when you're looking at a page full of questions; your mind is confused and full of random thoughts, and the clock is ticking down faster than you would like. Calm down and maintain the pace that you have set for yourself. Especially as you get down to the last few minutes of the test, don't let the small numbers on the clock make you panic. As long as you are on track by monitoring your pace, you are guaranteed to have time for each question.

⌀ DON'T RUSH

It is very easy to make errors when you are in a hurry. Maintaining a fast pace in answering questions is pointless if it makes you miss questions that you would have gotten right otherwise. Test writers like to include distracting information and wrong answers that seem right. Taking a little extra time to avoid careless mistakes can make all the difference in your test score. Find a pace that allows you to be confident in the answers that you select.

9

⊘ Keep Moving

Panicking will not help you pass the test, so do your best to stay calm and keep moving. Taking deep breaths and going through the answer elimination steps you practiced can help to break through a stress barrier and keep your pace.

Final Notes

The combination of a solid foundation of content knowledge and the confidence that comes from practicing your plan for applying that knowledge is the key to maximizing your performance on test day. As your foundation of content knowledge is built up and strengthened, you'll find that the strategies included in this chapter become more and more effective in helping you quickly sift through the distractions and traps of the test to isolate the correct answer.

Now that you're preparing to move forward into the test content chapters of this book, be sure to keep your goal in mind. As you read, think about how you will be able to apply this information on the test. If you've already seen sample questions for the test and you have an idea of the question format and style, try to come up with questions of your own that you can answer based on what you're reading. This will give you valuable practice applying your knowledge in the same ways you can expect to on test day.

Good luck and good studying!

Reading

Good reading skills are one of the most important things a person can have. If you don't master the art or reading, school will always be very hard for you, because school requires a lot of reading. If you don't read well, you will always struggle to make good grades. You will also miss out on one of life's great pleasures, because reading not only helps us learn, it's also a very enjoyable thing to do just for fun.

On the other hand, if you can read well, you can do well in school, and you can learn things easily in class or at home. The entire world opens up to good readers. You can choose from more classes, more things to do in your spare time, and more careers. You will have lots of things to talk about with people, and that can help you make friends. Life will be much more interesting and fun, in many different ways. So, work hard to improve your reading skills!

Practice Test

Reading

Questions 1-7 pertain to the following passage from The Wonderful Wizard of Oz by L. Frank Baum:

Dorothy carried the shoes into the house and placed them on the table. Then she came out again to the Munchkins and said: "I am anxious to get back to my aunt and uncle, for I am sure they will worry about me. Can you help me find my way?"

The Munchkins and the Witch first looked at one another, and then at Dorothy, and then shook their heads.

"At the East, not far from here," said one, "there is a great desert, and none could live to cross it."

"It is the same at the South," said another, "for I have been there and seen it. The South is the country of the Quadlings."

"I am told," said the third man, "that it is the same at the West. And that country, where the Winkies live, is ruled by the Wicked Witch of the West, who would make you her slave if you passed her way."

"The North is my home," said the old lady, "and at its edge is the same great desert that surrounds this Land of Oz. I'm afraid, my dear, you will have to live with us."

Dorothy began to sob at this, for she felt lonely among all these strange people. Her tears seemed to grieve the kind-hearted Munchkins, for they immediately took out their handkerchiefs and began to weep also. As for the little old woman, she took off her cap and balanced the point on the end of her nose, while she counted "One, two, three" in a solemn voice. At once the cap changed to a slate, on which was written in big, white chalk marks:

"LET DOROTHY GO TO THE CITY OF EMERALDS."

The little old woman took the slate from her nose, and having read the words on it, asked, "Is your name Dorothy, my dear?"

"Yes," answered the child, looking up and drying her tears.

"Then you must go to the City of Emeralds. Perhaps Oz will help you."

"Where is this city?" asked Dorothy.

"It is exactly in the center of the country, and is ruled by Oz, the Great izard I told you of."

"Is he a good man?" inquired the girl anxiously.

"He is a good Wizard. Whether he is a man or not I cannot tell, for I have never seen him."

12

"How can I get there?" asked Dorothy.

"You must walk. It is a long journey, through a country that is sometimes pleasant and sometimes dark and terrible. However, I will use all the magic arts I know of to keep you from harm."

"Won't you go with me?" pleaded the girl, who had begun to look upon the little old woman as her only friend.

"No, I cannot do that," she replied, "but I will give you my kiss, and no one will dare injure a person who has been kissed by the Witch of the North."

She came close to Dorothy and kissed her gently on the forehead. Where her lips touched the girl, they left a round, shining mark, as Dorothy found out soon after.

1. Where is Dorothy?
   a. Home
   b. The Land of Oz
   c. The City of Emeralds
   d. With her aunt and uncle

2. What does Dorothy want to do?
   a. Return to her aunt and uncle
   b. Live with the Witch of the North
   c. Stay in the Land of Oz
   d. Live in the City of Emeralds

3. How does Dorothy feel?
   a. Angry
   b. Happy
   c. Afraid
   d. Sad

4. How does the Witch of the North help Dorothy?
   a. She suggests that Dorothy live with the Munchkins and gives Dorothy her hat for protection.
   b. She suggests that Dorothy ask the Wizard of Oz for help and gives Dorothy a kiss for protection.
   c. She suggests that Dorothy should fly home and gives her a pair of shoes for protection.
   d. She suggests that Dorothy walk home and gives her a magic wand for protection.

5. Why does the Witch of the North suggest that Dorothy go to the City of Emeralds?
   a. To visit her aunt and uncle
   b. To visit the Witch of the North
   c. To ask the Wizard of Oz for help
   d. To ask the Witch of the North for help

6. What does the word *weep* mean in this sentence?

> "Her tears seemed to grieve the kind-hearted Munchkins, for they immediately took out their handkerchiefs and began to weep also."

a. Cry
b. Blow their noses
c. Laugh
d. Frown

7. What does the word *pleasant* mean in this sentence?

> "You must walk. It is a long journey, through a country that is sometimes pleasant and sometimes dark and terrible. However, I will use all the magic arts I know of to keep you from harm."

a. Scary
b. Nice
c. Rough
d. Silly

Imagine that you are the author of The Wonderful Wizard of Oz. Your job is to add sentences to the paragraph below to continue Dorothy's story. For questions 8–12, choose the best sentences for this paragraph:

> "You must follow the yellow brick road to the City of Emeralds," the Witch of the North told Dorothy. "There you will find the help you need." Dorothy signaled to her little dog, Toto, to follow her as she placed her foot on the first yellow brick. The little girl knew that she had a long journey ahead of her. Dorothy and Toto started walking.

8. Choose the best sentence for the beginning of the paragraph to tell what Dorothy does first.

a. Dorothy and Toto walked all day and far into the night.
b. "How do I find the City of Emeralds?" Dorothy asked the Witch of the North.
c. Dorothy's feet were tired from walking, so she took off her shoes and waded in the water.
d. "Where should we sleep tonight?" Dorothy asked the Witch of the North.

9. Choose the best sentence to tell how Dorothy feels as she begins her journey to the City of Emeralds.

a. "I should pack some food for the journey," said Dorothy to Toto.
b. "The Munchkins are very kind," said Dorothy to the Witch of the North.
c. "The Witch of the North gave me a kiss," said Dorothy to her little black dog.
d. "Stay right beside me, Toto," said Dorothy nervously to her little black dog.

10. Choose the best sentence to describe what Dorothy sees during her journey.

a. Dorothy followed the yellow brick road through the green countryside dotted with little blue houses.
b. Dorothy was careful to follow the advice of the Witch of the North on her journey.
c. Dorothy was surprised that she didn't feel tired even though she had been walking for so long.
d. Dorothy was anxious to see her aunt and uncle again.

11. Choose the best sentence to tell what Dorothy does after she has been walking for a long time.

    a.   Dorothy kept walking with Toto right beside her.
    b.   Dorothy thanked the Munchkins for their help.
    c.   Finally, Dorothy came upon a shady tree and sat down under its leaves to rest.
    d.   Dorothy wondered how to find the City of Emeralds.

12. Choose the best concluding (end) sentence for the paragraph.

    a.   Dorothy decided to begin her journey.
    b.   Dorothy was tired after her long walk and soon fell asleep.
    c.   Dorothy and Toto said good-bye to the Witch of the North
    d.   Dorothy and Toto were nervous.

Questions 13-18 pertain to the following article:

Starting an Aquarium

Imagine bright green plants swaying back and forth in blue water. Add in a small castle and some colorful fish swimming around it. If this sounds like something you would enjoy having, you might want to start your own aquarium. An aquarium is a tank filled with water and plants where you can keep fish. Aquarium fish are easy pets to take care of, if you are careful to choose the right fish and the right aquarium equipment.

Aquarium fish can be divided into four groups: tropical freshwater species, tropical marine species, coldwater freshwater species, and coldwater marine species. Tropical freshwater species are the easiest fish to keep because their needs change based on their surroundings and the resources they have available. They are able to adapt to living in different environments. Some tropical freshwater fish are the rosy barb, angelfish, and x-ray fish.

Below is a list of things to remember when you are setting up an aquarium:

- Choose your fish first. This will tell you what type of tank, water, and plants you need.
- Find out how your fish live in the wild. If the type of fish you chose normally live in schools, or groups, that means they are social fish. You will need to buy more than one of that kind to keep your fish from being lonely.
- Find out what your fish eat. Different fish need different types of food.

13. What is the main idea of this article?

    a.   How to choose a pet
    b.   How to set up an aquarium
    c.   How to tell the difference between angelfish and x-ray fish
    d.   How to identify different species of fish

14. What does the author say is the easiest group of fish to take care of?

    a.   Tropical freshwater species
    b.   Tropical marine species
    c.   Coldwater freshwater species
    d.   Coldwater marine species

15. What is the first thing you need to do when starting an aquarium?

a. Get fish food
b. Buy a tank
c. Buy plants and a castle
d. Choose your fish

16. An angelfish is a type of _____.

a. Coldwater freshwater species
b. Coldwater marine species
c. Tropical freshwater species
d. Tropical marine species

17. What does the word adapt mean in this sentence?

"They are able to adapt to living in different environments."

a. To improve
b. To change in order to fit in
c. To move forward
d. To make friends

18. Which of the following would be the best question to ask the author of this article?

a. What kind of dog should I choose for a pet, and are dogs easy to take care of?
b. Why do some fish swim together in schools?
c. If my fish usually live in schools, how many of that kind do I need?
d. How do fish breathe underwater?

You have been asked to write a report about butterflies. Information about butterflies is given below. For questions 19–24, choose the best sentences to write a paragraph about butterflies for your report.

Information about butterflies:

- Butterflies have thousands of tiny scales on their wings.
- A caterpillar changes into a butterfly during a process called metamorphosis.
- Butterflies are insects.
- Butterflies drink through a narrow tube in their mouths called a proboscis.
- Some butterflies are poisonous to eat.
- Butterflies have beautiful colors and patterns on their wings.
- A Monarch and a Pipevine Swallowtail are two examples of butterflies that are poisonous to eat.
- Metamorphosis is when a caterpillar changes into a chrysalis and then an adult butterfly.
- Butterflies like to drink flower nectar.
- A butterfly has a thin body and four wings.

19. Choose the best topic sentence for this paragraph.

a. A Monarch butterfly is poisonous to eat.
b. Butterflies are interesting and beautiful insects.
c. Some people collect butterflies.
d. Butterflies go through a process called metamorphosis.

20. Choose the sentence that gives the best definition of a butterfly.

- a. A butterfly is an insect with a thin body and four wings.
- b. A butterfly drinks flower nectar.
- c. A butterfly is an insect that can fly.
- d. A caterpillar changes into a butterfly during metamorphosis.

21. Choose the best sentence to follow this sentence: A Pipevine Swallowtail butterfly is poisonous to eat.

- a. Butterflies have thousands of tiny, colored scales on their wings.
- b. A Monarch and a Pipevine Swallowtail are two examples of butterflies.
- c. During metamorphosis, a caterpillar is transformed into a butterfly.
- d. Another example of a butterfly that is poisonous to eat is a Monarch butterfly.

22. Choose the sentence that gives the most information about the life cycle of a butterfly.

- a. A caterpillar changes into a butterfly during a process called metamorphosis.
- b. A butterfly is an insect with a thin body and four wings.
- c. During a process called metamorphosis, a caterpillar changes into a chrysalis and then an adult butterfly.
- d. Butterflies like to eat flower nectar.

23. Choose the sentence that gives the most information about a butterfly's eating habits.

- a. Butterflies drink flower nectar.
- b. A butterfly drinks flower nectar through a tube in its mouth called a proboscis.
- c. A butterfly has a narrow tube in its mouth called a proboscis.
- d. Some butterflies are poisonous to eat.

24. Choose the best concluding (end) sentence for the paragraph.

- a. Butterflies are interesting insects that some people collect.
- b. Butterflies like the Monarch and Pipevine Swallowtail are poisonous to eat.
- c. Butterflies are insects that begin life as caterpillars, change through metamorphosis, and eat flower nectar through a tube called a proboscis.
- d. People can create a butterfly garden by growing flowering plants that butterflies like.

You have been asked to give an oral report in front of your class about the life of President Abraham Lincoln. Answer questions 25–28 by making the best choices to prepare your report.

25. Which of the following would be the best resource for information about Abraham Lincoln's life?

- a. Dictionary
- b. Thesaurus
- c. Fiction (made up) short story
- d. Nonfiction (true) biography

26. Look at the categories below. How would you organize your report on Abraham Lincoln?

- a. Childhood, Adulthood, Favorite Foods
- b. Childhood, Adulthood, Greatest Accomplishments
- c. Childhood, Education, Family
- d. Childhood, Favorite Foods, Hobbies

27. Which of the following sentences about Abraham Lincoln belongs in the Childhood category?
   a. Abraham Lincoln was born on February 12, 1809.
   b. Abraham Lincoln was the sixteenth president of the United States of America.
   c. Abraham Lincoln died when he was only fifty-six years old.
   d. President Lincoln signed the Emancipation Proclamation on January 1, 1863.

28. Which of the following graphics would be the best choice to use during your report?
   a. Bar graph showing the number of Abraham Lincoln's supporters
   b. T-chart of the pros and cons of being president
   c. Pie chart of the amount of votes Abraham Lincoln received from each state when he was elected president
   d. Timeline of events in Abraham Lincoln's life

For questions 29–34, choose the word or words that best complete(s) each sentence:

29. "I don't like being the center of attention. I can't get up and speak in front of all of those people," Peter _____.
   a. exclaimed excitedly
   b. questioned eagerly
   c. stammered nervously
   d. shouted angrily

30. The movie, _____ was about a baseball player, started late.
   a. that
   b. which
   c. who
   d. whose

31. I _____ taking the bus to school tomorrow.
   a. was
   b. will be
   c. won't
   d. would

32. Our class is taking a _____ trip on _____.
   a. Field, Friday
   b. field, friday
   c. Field, friday
   d. field, Friday

33. The bookshelf was _____ high for Daniel _____ reach.
   a. to, too
   b. too, to
   c. two, to
   d. too, two

34. We are going on our family _____ in _____.

    a. vacation, January
    b. vaction, Janaury
    c. vacation, january
    d. vacation, Janaury

For questions 35–37, choose the sentence with the correct punctuation:

35.

    a. "May I go to the movies with John tomorrow?" Sam asked his mom.
    b. May I go to the movies with John tomorrow? Sam asked his mom.
    c. "May I go to the movies with John tomorrow? Sam asked his mom."
    d. "May I go to the movies with John tomorrow" Sam asked his mom?

36.

    a. Molly, watch out for the runaway train.
    b. Molly, watch out for the runaway train?
    c. Molly, watch out for the runaway train!
    d. Molly, watch out for the runaway train,

37.

    a. Maria wanted to give a party for her mom and she wanted it to be a surprise.
    b. Maria wanted to give a party for her mom; and she wanted it to be a surprise.
    c. Maria wanted to give a party for her mom. and she wanted it to be a surprise.
    d. Maria wanted to give a party for her mom, and she wanted it to be a surprise.

38. Read the sentences. Choose the word that is an antonym (opposite) of the word ally.

Janet was happy to have Noah on her team. It felt great to have him as an ally.

    a. Friend
    b. Enemy
    c. Teammate
    d. Coach

39. Read the sentence. Choose the meaning of the word protested.

"You can't take away recess!" Lynn protested to her teacher.

    a. Spoke strongly in favor
    b. Spoke in a friendly way
    c. Spoke strongly against
    d. Spoke in a careless way

40. Read the sentences. Choose the meaning of the word boast.

Julian told everyone that he scored the winning goal for his soccer team. His mother had to remind him that it is not polite to boast.

    a. Talk too much
    b. Score a goal
    c. Improve your soccer skills
    d. Brag about your accomplishments

41. Read the sentence. Choose the answer that best describes the meaning of the sentence.

Friends are the flowers in the garden of life.

a. We should be friends with people who grow flowers.
b. Friends bring color and happiness into our lives.
c. Friends are people who bring us flowers.
d. We should ask our friends to garden with us.

42. Read the sentence. Choose the answer that best describes the meaning of the sentence.

Look before you leap.

a. Always think about your actions before doing anything.
b. Always look at the other side of a bridge before crossing it.
c. Always look before jumping into a swimming pool.
d. Always stop and look before crossing the street.

Written Expression

The ability to express your thoughts clearly in writing is one of the most important skills a person can have. Whether a person is writing to a friend, a coworker, or even the President, they must be able to communicate their message clearly. The same is true of understanding things written by others. Effective reading depends on a clear understanding of what's being read.

For questions 1 - 4, fill in the blank with the correct relative pronoun or relative adverb.

1. _____ wants my old baseball glove can have it.

2. Do you remember _____ you put the mop bucket?

3. This is my classmate _____ I told you about.

4. I can't wait until the day _____ I turn 16.

Present progressive tense: this is used when a verb describes an action that is continuous, and is going on right now:

The teacher is grading the tests.

Past progressive tense: this tense is used when you're talking about something that was happening in the past. Often it's used to describe something that was happening when something else happened.

The teacher was grading the tests last night.

The teacher was grading the tests when the fire alarm went off.

Future progressive tense: this tense is used for an action that will happen in the future and is an ongoing action.

The teacher will be grading the tests while the students are at gym class.

I will be doing my homework after school.

Progressive Tense Exercises

Rewrite these two sentences in present progressive tense.

5. I ride my bike.

_____

6. I play chess.

_____

Rewrite these two sentence pairs. Combine them into one sentence using the past progressive tense.

7. We studied for the test. We didn't want to fail.

_____

8. We read quietly. The teacher announced a surprise quiz.

_____

In these two sentences, fill in the blank spaces with the future progressive tense of the verb shown in parentheses.

9. Which teams (play) _____ _____ _____ for the championship?

10. I (study) _____ _____ _____ _____ _____ all night long.

For the next two questions, look at the word in front of each sentence. Fill in the blank space in each sentence with a modal verb to express that thought.

11. ABILITY: Our music teacher says Mark _____ play

the piano better than anyone else in my class.

12. CERTAINTY: Doug has never missed a day of

school before, so he _____ be really sick.

For the next two questions, read each passage, and then choose the correct order of adjectives from the choices below the passage. If you think the passage already has the adjectives in the correct order, choose NO CHANGE.

13. the yellow new big bus
   a. NO CHANGE
   b. the new yellow big bus
   c. the big yellow new bus
   d. the big new yellow bus

14. the Canadian old hilarious clown
   a. NO CHANGE
   b. the Canadian hilarious old clown
   c. the hilarious old Canadian clown
   d. the old Canadian hilarious clown

For the next two questions, circle the preposition in each sentence.

15. Kids, I want you home by lunchtime!

16. What do you think we should do regarding the missing cupcake?

For the next two questions, circle the prepositional phrase in each sentence. Then decide if the prepositional phrase is functioning as an adjective, or as an adverb. Write ADJ at the end of the sentence if it's an adjective phrase; write ADV at the end of the sentence if it's an adverb phrase.

17. Let's play volleyball after lunch. ____

18. Except for Lawanda, the entire class failed the spelling test. ____

For the next two questions, decide if you're reading a complete sentence, or a sentence fragment. If it's a complete sentence, write C in the blank space. If it's a sentence fragment, write F in the blank space.

22

19. Hurry up! ____

20. Until it's time to go to bed. ____

For the next two questions, decide if you're reading a complete sentence, or a run-on sentence. If it's a complete sentence, write C in the blank space. If it's a run-on sentence, write R in the blank space.

21. Billy is in fourth grade and he likes pancakes and he likes football and he speaks Spanish. ____

22. It's starting to rain; we should go inside. ____

For the next two questions, circle the word on the right that belongs in the blank space.

23. I received a ribbon from the _____ for perfect attendance.

principal   principle

24. They are running late because _____ car had a flat tire.

they're   their   there

For the next two questions: read each sentence or phrase, and then rewrite it to say the same thing with fewer words.

25. I arrive at school every weekday, Monday through Friday, at 8 AM in the morning.

_____

26. In the event that it starts raining all of a sudden, we'll go inside.

_____

27. Which word is usually a negative synonym for *helper*?

   a. accomplice
   b. aide
   c. assistant
   d. partner

28. Which word would let a reader know that something is extremely *cold*?

   a. cool
   b. frosty
   c. chilly
   d. frigid

In each of the next two sentences, there is a simile or metaphor. Circle it, and in the blank line below the sentence, write in your own words what point the writer is making with the simile or metaphor.

29. Quiet, mild-mannered Trent turns into a bulldozer on the football field.

_____

23

34. Winning the spelling bee was like a dream come true.

_____

Each of the next two items contains a common idiom. In the blank line below it, explain what the idiom means.

31. raining cats and dogs

_____

32. hit the sack

_____

Fill in the blank space with the word or phrase to complete each proverb.

33. When the cat's away,

_____.

34. Don't count your chickens

_____.

For the next four items, read each word, then find its antonym in the box at the top, and write it in the blank space next to the word.

shame	stingy	close	inferior	clumsy
seldom	weakness	temporary	slow	hideous
boring	loyalty	liquid	dislike	failure
organized	friendly	dull	folly	rare

35. beautiful _____
36. superior _____
37. common _____
38. generous _____

Mathematics

Math is one of the most important things you'll learn in school. That doesn't mean it has to be boring, though. Learning math can be enjoyable. Answer the questions in the first part of this lesson, and then take the test at the end to see how you're doing in math.

 The place value of a digit is determined by where it is in a number.

Hundred Thousands	Ten Thousands	Thousands	Hundreds	Tens	Ones
1	2	3	4	5	6

1 2 3, 4 5 6

One Hundred Twenty Three Thousand, Four Hundred Fifty Six

Write these numbers correctly in the blanks.

1. 422,719 =

4	2	2	7	1	9
Hundred Thousands	Ten Thousands	Thousands	Hundreds	Tens	Ones

2. 982,124 =

Hundred Thousands	Ten Thousands	Thousands	Hundreds	Tens	Ones

3. 263,927 =

Hundred Thousands	Ten Thousands	Thousands	Hundreds	Tens	Ones

4. 627,141 =

Hundred Thousands	Ten Thousands	Thousands	Hundreds	Tens	Ones

5. 891,362 =

Hundred Thousands	Ten Thousands	Thousands	Hundreds	Tens	Ones

Solve the word problems below.

1. In the number 25,483 :
   A. This digit is in the ones place _____
   B. This digit is in the hundreds place _____
   C. The 5 is in the _____ place
   D. The 8 is in the _____ place

2. In the number 62,134 :
   A. This digit is in the tens place _____
   B. This digit is in the thousands place _____
   C. The 6 is in the _____ place
   D. The 4 is in the _____ place

3. In the number 84,327 :
   A. This digit is in the ones place _____
   B. This digit is in the thousands place _____
   C. The 2 is in the _____ place
   D. The 8 is in the _____ place

4. In the number 14,960 :
   A. This digit is in the hundreds place _____
   B. This digit is in the ten-thousands place _____
   C. The 0 is in the _____ place
   D. The 4 is in the _____ place

5. In the number 40,589 :
   A. This digit is in the ones place _____
   B. This digit is in the hundreds place _____
   C. The 0 is in the _____ place
   D. The 4 is in the _____ place

Solve the problems below using regrouping.

1. 6 8,5 0 2
    + 3 5,8 4 7
    ‾‾‾‾‾‾‾‾‾‾

2. 3 2,0 0 0
    + 1 7,8 1 5
    ‾‾‾‾‾‾‾‾‾‾

3. 4 9,2 1 5
    + 2 1,5 8 9
    ‾‾‾‾‾‾‾‾‾‾

4. 6 5,1 0 7
    + 4 2,2 3 8
    ‾‾‾‾‾‾‾‾‾‾

5. 8 6,0 1 1
    + 3 2,9 9 7
    ‾‾‾‾‾‾‾‾‾‾

6. 9 1,0 5 8
    + 1 5,2 1 1
    ‾‾‾‾‾‾‾‾‾‾

7. 7 0,1 2 2
    + 6 2,9 3 9
    ‾‾‾‾‾‾‾‾‾‾

8. 2 9,0 0 6
    + 1 1,2 7 1
    ‾‾‾‾‾‾‾‾‾‾

9. 5 5,1 2 7
    + 1 7,5 6 8
    ‾‾‾‾‾‾‾‾‾‾

10. 2 5,0 8 7
    +   9,1 7 5
    ‾‾‾‾‾‾‾‾‾‾

11. 4 9,1 8 6
    + 2 3,2 5 0
    ‾‾‾‾‾‾‾‾‾‾

12. 9 5,1 1 8
    +   3,9 3 5
    ‾‾‾‾‾‾‾‾‾‾

13. 7 7,1 1 7
    + 5 9,9 9 0
    ‾‾‾‾‾‾‾‾‾‾

14. 4 5,7 1 0
    + 3 6,3 0 3
    ‾‾‾‾‾‾‾‾‾‾

15. 6 7,1 8 1
    +   2,6 2 8
    ‾‾‾‾‾‾‾‾‾‾

16. 8 2,2 0 7
    + 6 0,8 4 5
    ‾‾‾‾‾‾‾‾‾‾

17. 4 5,3 8 7
    + 3 6,1 0 5
    ‾‾‾‾‾‾‾‾‾‾

18. 7 7,0 0 7
    + 1 1,3 6 7
    ‾‾‾‾‾‾‾‾‾‾

19. 6 0,1 1 7
    + 4 6,2 8 9
    ‾‾‾‾‾‾‾‾‾‾

20. 8 4,9 9 9
    + 2 6,1 1 1
    ‾‾‾‾‾‾‾‾‾‾

Use what you learned about borrowing to
solve the problems below.

1. 3,2 9 1
   − 1,6 7 5

2. 7,0 5 2
   − 5,8 9 4

3. 1,0 2 0
   −   5 3 2

4. 9,2 1 4
   − 7,5 8 0

5. 2,8 5 6
   − 1,6 9 7

6. 5,4 4 1
   − 2,5 8 3

7. 7,6 5 4
   − 5,4 3 9

8. 9,2 0 1
   − 2,5 5 0

9. 6,5 4 9
   − 3,0 5 8

10. 1,2 0 5
    −   3 1 7

11. 4,0 5 3
    − 1,5 8 9

12. 9,0 8 7
    − 4,6 8 2

13. 3,0 0 1
    − 1,8 9 2

14. 9,8 9 7
    − 5,4 3 2

15. 6,9 0 1
    − 3,7 8 4

16. 5,3 3 8
    − 2,0 5 8

17. 8,0 7 1
    − 3,6 8 7

18. 9,0 0 1
    − 5,5 9 2

19. 4,2 0 7
    − 2,0 7 2

20. 9,9 9 1
    − 3,0 5 8

Find the totals below.

1. $6.05
 + $4.11

2. $3.94
 + $2.29

3. $9.99
 + $7.65

4. $5.25
 + $8.39

5. $8.38
 + $9.12

6. $66.45
 +$29.82

7. $95.30
 +$12.65

8. $84.94
 + $17.05

9. $29.75
    $1.40
 + $8.97

10. $20.51
    $45.68
 + $9.42

11. $95.12
    $58.63
 + $17.08

12. $62.22
    $30.52
 +$68.67

13. $152.78
   $126.36
 + $75.11

14. $429.33
   $639.95
 +$115.27

15. $290.24
   $907.57
 +$333.03

16. $369.67
   $105.18
 + $59.07

17. $625.99
   $470.75
 +$364.23

18. $129.00
   $650.70
 +$321.33

19. $459.99
   $630.01
 +$780.40

20. $111.27
   $252.96
 +$639.57

Use subtraction to solve the problems below.

1. Pete wants a new teddy bear. His mom is going to help him buy one. A new bear costs $19.50. Pete has $7.32. How much money does he need to get from mom?

_____

2. Tammy wants a new jump rope. She has $3.78. The jump rope costs $6.99. How much more money does she need?

_____

3. Randy and John want a new toy truck. The toy truck costs $13.75. Randy has $4.15 and John has $6.42. How much more money do they need?

_____

4. Eric sold his old pogo stick for $5.89. A new one costs $35.99. How much more money does Eric need?

_____

Solve the problems below.

1. 67
   x 49

2. 24
   x 15

3. 49
   x 36

4. 29
   x 27

5. 44
   x 39

6. 84
   x 60

7. 66
   x 34

8. 87
   x 11

9. 99
   x 49

10. 70
    x 59

11. 39
    x 27

12. 24
    x 17

13. 86
    x 37

14. 11
    x 83

15. 97
    x 57

16. 55
    x 90

17. 75
    x 22

18. 68
    x 43

19. 92
    x 37

20. 19
    x 26

Use division to solve the problems below.

1. Rachel bought three pairs of ballet shoes for $99. What is the cost of each pair of shoes?

_____

2. Charlie has 21 kids in his class. If he divides the kids into 3 groups how many kids will be in each group?

_____

3. Sara loves her dolls; she has 12 of them. If she divides them into groups of 4, how many dolls will be in each group?

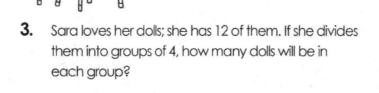

4. Harry has 72 toy trucks and cars. If he divides them into groups of 8, how many cars and trucks will be in each group?

_____

Mometrix

Identify each shape below and write the names in the blanks.

1.

cube

2.

_____

3.

_____

4.

_____

5.

_____

6.

_____

7.

_____

8.

_____

9.

_____

10.

_____

11.

_____

12.

_____

13.

_____

14.

_____

15.

_____

16.

_____

33

Area is the measurement of a shape's surface area.
To find the **area** of a shape, multiply the length by the width.

24 ft.

8 ft.

Area = 24 ft. x 8 ft. = 192 ft.
Area = 192 sq. ft.

Find the area of each shape. Write the problem out.

1.   6 in.

6 in.

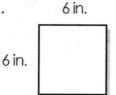

2.   3 ft.

12 ft.

3.

21 in.   21 in.

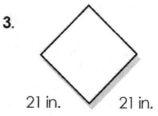

6 x 6 = 36 sq. in.

_____   _____

4.   4 ft.

25 ft.

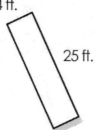

5.

12 yd.   12 yd.

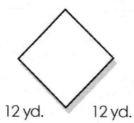

6.   9 in.

9 in.

_____   _____   _____

Volume is the number of cubic units that can fit into a shape. To find volume, count the cubes or multiply length times width times height. *(L x W x H = volume)*

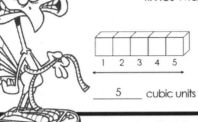

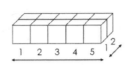

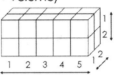

_____5_____ cubic units   __5 x 2 = 10__ cubic units   __5 x 2 x 2 = 20__ cubic units

Find the volume of the shapes below.

1.

__5 x 2 x 2 = 20__ cubic units

2.

_____ cubic units

3.

_____ cubic units

4.

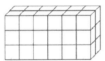

_____ cubic units

5.

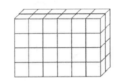

_____ cubic units

6.

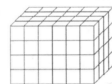

_____ cubic units

7.

_____ cubic units

8.

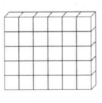

_____ cubic units

9.

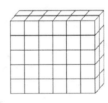

_____ cubic units

One - half pound (lb.) = 8 ounces (oz.)
1 pound (lb.) = 16 ounces (oz.)
One - half ton (T.) = 1,000 pounds (lb.)
1 ton (T.) = 2,000 pounds (lb.)

Complete the problems below.

 **1.** 48 oz. = __3__ lb.

 2. 32 lb. = _____ oz.

 3. 4,000 lb. = _____ T.

 4. 80 oz. = _____ lb.

 5. 2 lb. = _____ oz.

 6. 8 lb. = _____ oz.

 7. 3T. = _____ lb.

 8. 6 lb. = _____ oz.

 9. 16 oz. = _____ lb.

 **10.** 12,000 lb. = _____ T.

12 inches = 1 foot	3 feet = 1 yard
36 inches = 1 yard	

Compare inches to feet.

Use the symbols <, >, and = to answer the questions below

1. 10 feet **>** 100 inches
2. 20 inches ___ 3 feet
3. 12 inches ___ 1 foot
4. 6 feet ___ 50 inches
5. 40 inches ___ 3 feet
6. 5 feet ___ 70 inches
7. 4 feet ___ 48 inches
8. 72 inches ___ 6 feet

Compare inches, feet, and yards.

Use the symbols <, >, and = to answer the questions below

9. 9 feet ___ 32 yards
10. 46 inches ___ 2 yards
11. 40 feet ___ 3 yards
12. 4 yards ___ 15 feet
13. 4 feet ___ 100 inches
14. 1 foot ___ 2 yards
15. 24 inches ___ 1 foot
16. 6 yards ___ 24 feet

| 2 Cups = 1 Pint | 2 Pints = 1 Quart | 4 Quarts = 1 Gallon |

1 Cup   1 Pint   1 Quart   1 Gallon

Circle the number of objects to match the amount in the box.

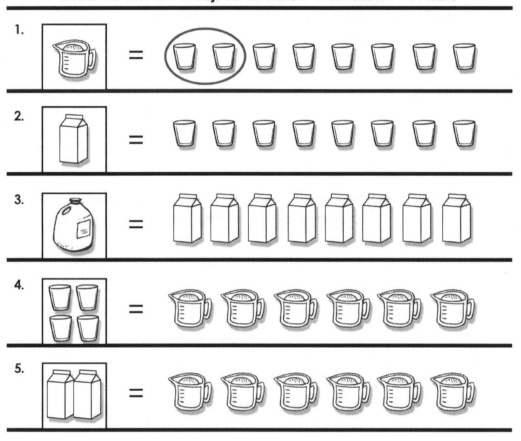

1.

2.

3.

4.

5.

38

A **mixed number** is a number written as a whole number and a fraction.

When subtracting mixed numbers with common denominators, subtract the whole numbers first, then subtract the numerators. The denominators will remain the same.

$$9\frac{5}{6} - 4\frac{2}{6} = 5\frac{3}{6}$$ ← Numerator
← Denominator

Subtract the mixed numbers below.

1. $6\frac{3}{4}$
   $- 4\frac{1}{4}$
   _____
   $2\frac{2}{4}$

2. $8\frac{4}{6}$
   $- 3\frac{2}{6}$
   _____

3. $5\frac{8}{9}$
   $- 2\frac{7}{9}$
   _____

4. $9\frac{11}{13}$
   $- 8\frac{9}{13}$
   _____

5. $32\frac{15}{21}$
   $-18\frac{5}{21}$
   _____

6. $12\frac{7}{30}$
   $- 2\frac{2}{30}$
   _____

7. $17\frac{20}{26}$
   $-11\frac{12}{26}$
   _____

8. $25\frac{13}{17}$
   $-18\frac{8}{17}$
   _____

- Reducing (or simplifying) fractions means reducing a fraction to the lowest possible terms.
  - To do this, find a number that both the numerator and the denominator of the fraction are divisible by. Use that number as the numerator and denominator of a new fraction equal to one. Then divide the fractions.

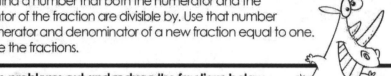

Write the problems out and reduce the fractions below.

1. $\dfrac{9}{18} \div \underline{\hspace{1cm}} = \underline{\hspace{1cm}}$

2. $\dfrac{6}{28} \div \underline{\hspace{1cm}} = \underline{\hspace{1cm}}$

3. $\dfrac{15}{18} \div \underline{\hspace{1cm}} = \underline{\hspace{1cm}}$

4. $\dfrac{12}{16} \div \underline{\hspace{1cm}} = \underline{\hspace{1cm}}$

5. $\dfrac{18}{36} \div \underline{\hspace{1cm}} = \underline{\hspace{1cm}}$

6. $\dfrac{24}{75} \div \underline{\hspace{1cm}} = \underline{\hspace{1cm}}$

7. $\dfrac{7}{49} \div \underline{\hspace{1cm}} = \underline{\hspace{1cm}}$

8. $\dfrac{27}{81} \div \underline{\hspace{1cm}} = \underline{\hspace{1cm}}$

ANSWERS

Place Value and Number Sense

1.

4	2	2	7	1	9
Hundred Thousands	Ten Thousands	Thousands	Hundreds	Tens	Ones

2.

9	8	2	1	2	4
Hundred Thousands	Ten Thousands	Thousands	Hundreds	Tens	Ones

3.

2	6	3	9	2	7
Hundred Thousands	Ten Thousands	Thousands	Hundreds	Tens	Ones

4.

6	2	7	1	4	1
Hundred Thousands	Ten Thousands	Thousands	Hundreds	Tens	Ones

5.

8	9	1	3	6	2
Hundred Thousands	Ten Thousands	Thousands	Hundreds	Tens	Ones

1. a. 3

b. 4

c. thousands

d. tens

2. a. 3

b. 2

c. ten thousands

d. ones

3. a. 7

b. 4

c. tens

d. ten thousands

4. a. 9

b. 1

c. ones

d. thousands

5. a. 9

b. 5

c. thousands

d. ten thousands

Addition

1. 104,349

2. 49,815

3. 70,804

4. 107,345

5. 119,008

6. 106,269

7. 133,061

8. 40,277

9. 72,695

10. 34,262

11. 72,436

12. 99,053

13. 137,107

14. 82,013

15. 69,809

16. 143,052

17. 81,492

18. 88,374

19. 106,406

20. 111,110

Subtraction

1. 1,616

2. 1,158

3. 488

4. 1,634

5. 1,159

6. 2,858

7. 2,215

8. 6,651

9. 3,491

10. 888

11. 2,464

12. 4,405

13. 1,109

14. 4,465

15. 3,117

16. 3,280

17. 4,384

18. 3,409

19. 2,135

20. 6,933

Decimals

1. $10.16

2. $6.23

3. $17.64

4. $13.64

5. $17.50

6. $96.27

7. $107.95

8. $101.99

9. $40.12

10. $75.61

11. $170.83

12. $161.41

13. $354.25

14. $1,184.55

15. $1,530.84

16. $533.92

17. $1,460.97

18. $1,101.03

19. $1,870.40

20. $1,003.80

1. $12.18

2. $3.21

3. $3.18

4. $30.10

Multiplication

1. 3,283

2. 360

3. 1,764

4. 783

5. 1,716

6. 5,040

7. 2,244

8. 957

9. 4,851

10. 4,130

11. 1,053

12. 408

13. 3,182

14. 913

15. 5,529

16. 4,950

17. 1,650

18. 2,924

19. 3,404

20. 494

Division

1. $33

2. 7 kids

3. 3 dolls

4. 9 cars and trucks

Geometry

1. cube

2. cylinder

3. sphere

4. prism

5. pyramid

6. cuboid

7. cone

8. cube

9. sphere

10. prism

11. cuboid

12. cone

13. cylinder

14. pyramid

15. cube

16. prism

1. 36 sq. in

2. 36 sq. ft

3. 441 sq. in

4. 100 sq. ft

5. 144 sq. yd

6. 81 sq. in

1. 20

2. 30

3. 24

4. 36

5. 48

6. 96

7. 24

8. 30

9. 60

Measurements

1. 3 lb

2. 512 oz

3. 2 T

4. 5 lb

5. 32 oz

6. 128 oz

7. 6,000 lb

8. 96 oz

9. 1 lb

10. 6 T

1. >

2. <

3. =

4. >

5. >

6. <

7. =

8. =

9. <

10. <

11. >

12. <

13. <

14. <

15. >

16. <

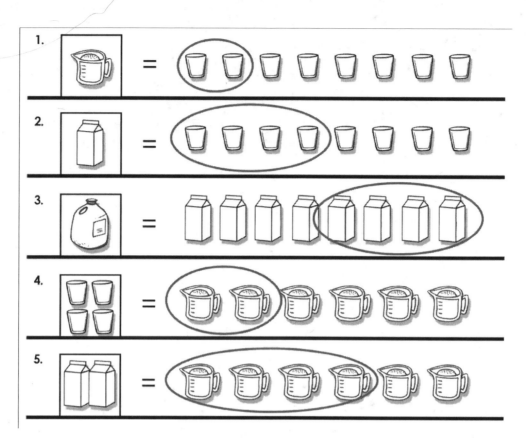

Fractions

1. $2\frac{2}{4}$

2. $5\frac{2}{6}$

3. $3\frac{1}{9}$

4. $1\frac{2}{13}$

5. $1\frac{10}{21}$

6. $10\frac{5}{30}$

7. $6\frac{8}{26}$

8. $7\frac{5}{17}$

1. $\frac{9}{9}$ and $\frac{1}{2}$

2. $\frac{2}{2}$ and $\frac{3}{14}$

3. $\frac{3}{3}$ and $\frac{5}{6}$

4. $\frac{4}{4}$ and $\frac{3}{4}$

5. $\frac{18}{18}$ and $\frac{1}{2}$

6. $\frac{3}{3}$ and $\frac{8}{25}$

7. $\frac{7}{7}$ and $\frac{1}{7}$

8. $\frac{27}{27}$ and $\frac{1}{3}$

Mathematics

1. Which statement is false?

    a. 7 pens of 3 cattle is 20 cattle.
    b. 8 pens of 3 cattle is 24 cattle.
    c. 3 containers filled with 8 pencils is 24 pencils.
    d. 3 containers filled with 7 pencils is 21 pencils.

2. Johnny just spent $4.50 on 18 erasers. How much does one eraser cost?

    a. $0.20
    b. $0.25
    c. $0.30
    d. $0.35

3. Raquel has 36 stamps. She groups the stamps into 9 equal groups. She then adds two more stamps to each group. If she gives 4 stamps to each of her 13 friends, how many stamps will she have left?

    a. 0
    b. 1
    c. 2
    d. 3

4. The numbers 4, 6, and 10 are all factors of which number?

    a. 12
    b. 24
    c. 60
    d. 80

5. Which pattern of numbers describes the number of line segments needed in the shape pattern listed below?

   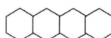

    a. 1, 2, 3, 4
    b. 6, 12, 18, 24
    c. 6, 10, 14, 18
    d. 6, 11, 16, 21

6. Which of the following statements is true?

    a. 800 is ten times greater than 8.
    b. 3000 is ten times greater than 30.
    c. 70 is ten times greater than 700.
    d. 900 is ten times greater than 90.

7. Which of the following is the written form for the number 5,320,080?

    a. five million, thirty-two thousand, eighty
    b. five million, three hundred twenty thousand, eighty
    c. five million, three hundred twenty thousand, eight
    d. five thousand, three hundred twenty-eight

8. Which of the following is 7,859 rounded to the hundreds place?

    a. 7,850
    b. 7,860
    c. 7,800
    d. 7,900

9. Evaluate 452 + 388 =

    a. 740
    b. 840
    c. 830
    d. 930

10. Evaluate 1250 − 487 =

    a. 837
    b. 737
    c. 763
    d. 863

11. What is the area of the figure below?

14 units

32 units

    a. 448 square units
    b. 46 square units
    c. 92 square units
    d. 348 square units

12. Evaluate 457 × 7 =

    a. 3199
    b. 2869
    c. 2899
    d. 3189

13. Evaluate 8621 ÷ 6 =

    a. 1435 r 5
    b. 1013 r 3
    c. 1535 r 0
    d. 1436 r 5

14. Which fraction model is *not* equivalent to $\frac{3}{5}$?

a.

b.

c.

d.

15. Which of the following fractions is equivalent to $\frac{6}{18}$?

a. $\frac{2}{6}$

b. $\frac{2}{3}$

c. $\frac{1}{5}$

d. $\frac{2}{9}$

16. Fill in the blank with the appropriate symbol: $\frac{2}{3}$ —— $\frac{3}{5}$.

a. >

b. <

c. =

d. Cannot be determined

17. Fill in the blank with the appropriate symbol: $\frac{3}{8}$ —— $\frac{2}{5}$.

a. >

b. <

c. =

d. Cannot be determined

18. Which equation is represented by the following model?

a. $\frac{9}{4} + \frac{4}{4} = \frac{13}{4}$

b. $\frac{7}{16} + \frac{4}{16} = \frac{11}{16}$

c. $\frac{9}{16} + \frac{4}{16} = \frac{13}{16}$

d. $\frac{9}{16} + \frac{12}{16} = \frac{21}{16}$

52

19. Which of the following expressions is not equal to $\frac{5}{8}$?

    a. $\frac{8}{8} - \frac{1}{8} - \frac{1}{8} - \frac{1}{8} - \frac{1}{8}$

    b. $\frac{2}{8} + \frac{2}{8} + \frac{1}{8}$

    c. $\frac{1}{8} + \frac{1}{8} + \frac{1}{8} + \frac{1}{8} + \frac{1}{8}$

    d. $\frac{1}{8} + \frac{2}{8} + \frac{3}{8} + \frac{4}{8} - \frac{5}{8}$

20. Evaluate $4\frac{1}{5} + 3\frac{2}{5} =$

    a. $7\frac{3}{10}$

    b. $7\frac{3}{5}$

    c. $7\frac{1}{5}$

    d. $7\frac{2}{5}$

21. Evaluate $11\frac{3}{5} - 8\frac{2}{5} =$

    a. $2\frac{4}{5}$

    b. $3\frac{4}{5}$

    c. $2\frac{1}{5}$

    d. $3\frac{1}{5}$

22. Jordan is making a cake. He wants to reduce the amount of sugar in the recipe. If the original recipe calls for $2\frac{1}{3}$ cups of sugar and he wants to decrease it by $\frac{2}{3}$ cup of sugar, how many cups of sugar should Jordan put into the recipe?

    a. 1 cup

    b. $1\frac{1}{3}$ cups

    c. $1\frac{2}{3}$ cups

    d. 2 cups

23. A cuckoo clock is being built and the pendulum of the clock needs to be cut from a piece of wood so that it is $\frac{1}{12}$ meter. If you are going to build 5 cuckoo clocks, what will the total length of 5 pendulums be?

    a. $\frac{5}{12}$ meter

    b. $\frac{1}{60}$ meter

    c. $5\frac{1}{12}$ meters

    d. $\frac{1}{2}$ meter

24. Evaluate $4 \times \frac{3}{5} =$

    a. $\frac{7}{5}$

    b. $\frac{3}{20}$

    c. $\frac{1}{3}$

    d. $\frac{12}{5}$

25. Which equation represents the fraction model shown?

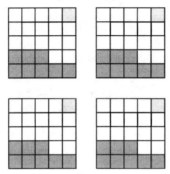

    a. $4 \times \frac{4}{5} = \frac{16}{5}$

    b. $4 \times \frac{8}{25} = \frac{32}{25}$

    c. $4 \times \frac{1}{2} = 2$

    d. $4 \times \frac{9}{25} = \frac{36}{25}$

26. While designing a tree fort, you want to have 9 pieces of rope that are $\frac{1}{2}$ meter to make a rope ladder. When you go to the store, how many meters of rope do you ask the clerk to sell you?

    a. 4 meters

    b. 9 meters

    c. $4\frac{1}{2}$ meters

    d. 18 meters

27. Add $\frac{7}{10} + \frac{57}{100}$.

    a. $\frac{127}{100}$

    b. $\frac{62}{100}$

    c. $\frac{64}{100}$

    d. $\frac{5770}{100}$

28. Rewrite $^{45}/_{100}$ **as a decimal.**

    a. 0.45

    b. 4.5

    c. 0.045

    d. 0.0045

29. Fill in the blank with the appropriate symbol to compare the following numbers: 0.24 0.18

    a.   <
    b.   >
    c.   =
    d.   Cannot be determined

30. You are deciding to go on a long distance bike ride. You ride a total of 3490 meters. Express this in kilometers.

    a.   349 kilometers
    b.   34900 kilometers
    c.   34.90 kilometers
    d.   3.490 kilometers

31. While you are working at a certain job, you are paid $40.25 per day. You work 5 days out of the week. You save $20 per week to buy a new bike. How much money do you have left over to spend at the end of the week?

    a. $181.25
    b. $59.75
    c. $101.25
    d. $25.25

32. A farmer is making a pen for his pigs. The model of the pen is to the right. What is the perimeter of the pen?

52 meters   18 meters

    a.   936 meters
    b.   70 meters
    c.   122 meters
    d.   140 meters

33. Richard and Mary are training for a race. On a particular day Richard runs $\frac{5}{8}$ of a mile and Mary runs $\frac{1}{2}$ of a mile. How much further did Richard run than Mary?

    a. $\frac{1}{2}$ mile
    b. $\frac{2}{3}$ mile
    c. $\frac{1}{4}$ mile
    d. $\frac{1}{8}$ mile

34. A one-degree angle is $\frac{1}{360}$ of a circle. 180 one-degree angles make up what fraction of a circle?

  a. $\frac{1}{4}$

  b. $\frac{1}{2}$

  c. $\frac{3}{4}$

  d. $\frac{4}{5}$

35. What is the measure of ∠ABC?

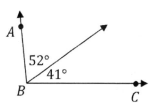

  a. 52°
  b. 41°
  c. 93°
  d. Cannot be determined

36. Measure the angle using a protractor.

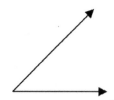

  a. 45°
  b. 90°
  c. 135°
  d. 180°

37. If $m\angle ABC = 100°$, what is $m\angle ABD$?

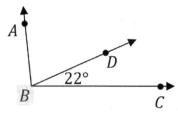

  a. 82°
  b. 122°
  c. 88°
  d. 78°

38. Classify the angle based on the measure of the angle.

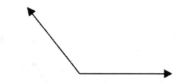

   a. Acute
   b. Obtuse
   c. Right
   d. Straight

39. Classify the figure.

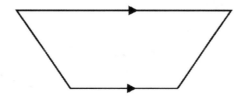

   a. Rhombus
   b. Trapezoid
   c. Kite
   d. Pentagon

40. Which of the following shapes do not have line symmetry?

a. 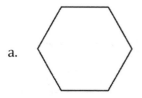   b.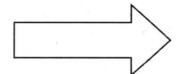

c. 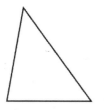   d.

Science

Learning about science is both fun and educational. The world is made up of all kinds of interesting plants and animals, in all shapes and sizes. We learn about these in science, and we also learn about things like stars and planets, weather, oceans, gravity, atoms, and much more. For many students, science is their favorite subject to study at school. Here are some questions about science that can help you improve your skills in this area.

1. What is the purpose of the pupil of the eye?
    a.   The pupil emits light to shine on objects you're looking at.
    b.   The pupil blocks light to prevent it from entering your eye.
    c.   The pupil is an opening through which light enters your eye.
    d.   The pupil exists so other creatures can see in which direction you're looking.

2. What is the term for the transparent front part of the eye?
    a.   Cochlea
    b.   Cornea
    c.   Iris
    d.   Retina

3. Clean panes of glass are so transparent that they are essentially invisible in the right lighting, which is why birds sometimes fly into them. Which of the following is the best explanation for why the glass can't be seen, but a similarly shaped metal sheet is easily visible?
    a.   The glass does not emit light.
    b.   The glass does not reflect light.
    c.   The glass emits the wrong kind of light, canceling visible light.
    d.   The glass reflects the wrong kind of light, canceling visible light.

Directions: Use the information below and your knowledge of science to answer questions 4 – 5.

Two nearby areas have the same kinds of rocks, but the soil has a different consistency in one area than in another. A geologist exploring the area theorizes that the difference is due to plants that exist in one area and not the other.

4. What is the best way to test the geologist's theory?
    a.   Dissect one of the plants.
    b.   Count the number of plants in the area.
    c.   Introduce some of the plants into a soil sample from the other area and see how the plants affect the soil.
    d.   There is no need to test; the geologist's theory is obviously wrong—living organisms cannot affect the soil.

5. There is an area downhill from the plants that has similar soil, even though there are no plants there. The geologist concludes that some of the soil may have been moved there from the uphill area. Which of the following processes is likely to have moved the soil?
    a.   Evaporation
    b.   Plate tectonics
    c.   Continental drift
    d.   Water runoff from rainfall

6. What is the term for the breakdown of rocks into soil and the motion of soil from one place to another as described above?
   a. Erosion
   b. Geology
   c. Glaciation
   d. Metamorphosis

7. What is the term for the height of a wave?
   a. Amplitude
   b. Frequency
   c. Intensity
   d. Power

8. If two waves in the ocean have the same height, can they be different in any other important way?
   a. No; two waves with the same height are essentially identical.
   b. Yes; they can have the same height but a different depth.
   c. Yes; they can have the same height but a different intensity.
   d. Yes; they can have the same height but a different wavelength.

9. A sailor dumps a barrel of toothpicks into the middle of the ocean. As the toothpicks are carried by the waves, which of the following best describes their motion?
   a. Each toothpick moves up and down, but it does not move in the direction of the wave.
   b. Each toothpick moves in the direction of the wave, but it does not move up and down.
   c. Each toothpick moves both up and down and in the direction of the wave.
   d. Some toothpicks move up and down, and some move in the direction of the wave.

10. Trees and many other plants have tissues inside called xylem and phloem that carry water and chemicals between different parts of the plant. The structure in a human that serves the most similar function to the xylem and phloem is/are the
   a. Tongue
   b. Skeleton
   c. Lungs
   d. Veins and arteries

11. Two otherwise similar species of plants have differently shaped and differently colored flowers. Which of the following is the most likely explanation for this?
   a. The flowers developed to absorb different nutrients.
   b. The flowers developed to attract different pollinators.
   c. The flowers developed to gather different amounts of light.
   d. The flowers developed to fend off different herbivores that would otherwise eat the plants.

12. A paleontologist discovers a fossil of a plant with large thorns. What can he probably conclude from this?
   a. The plant was carnivorous.
   b. The plant grew in a very dry area.
   c. The plant lived in an area with large herbivores.
   d. The plant grew in open fields with plenty of sunlight.

13. A scientist finds a plant with strange bulbs growing on it, and he wants to know what purpose the bulbs serve. Which of the following would best help him to find out?

 a. He could look for a similar-looking feature on other plants.
 b. He could transplant the plants into other areas and see if they grow differently.
 c. He could take the bulbs off some plants, keep the bulbs in a jar, and observe what happens to them.
 d. He could cut the bulbs off of some plants and evaluate how the plants without bulbs develop differently from plants with the bulbs left intact.

Directions: Use the information below and your knowledge of science to answer questions 14 – 16.

The following map (taken from the website of the NASA Earth Observatory) shows the location of major earthquakes in 2003.

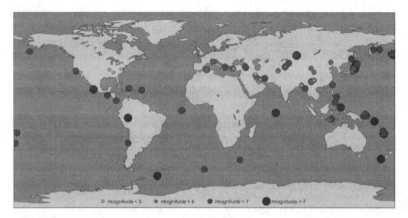

14. In which of the following continents did the *fewest* large earthquakes occur in 2003?

 a. Asia
 b. Australia
 c. Europe
 d. South America

15. Many of the earthquakes can be seen to have occurred along certain lines. What else is likely to be most common along those same lines?

 a. Canyons
 b. Cyclones
 c. Thunderstorms
 d. Volcanoes

16. The map shows several earthquakes occurring in the middle of the ocean. What can be caused by earthquakes on the ocean floor?

 a. Eclipses
 b. Hurricanes
 c. Monsoons
 d. Tsunamis

Directions: Use the information below and your knowledge of science to answer questions 17 – 19.

One ball is propelled toward another and collides with it. The following diagram shows the positions of the balls at various times before, during, and after the collision.

17. Which of the following statements is *not* supported by this experiment?

    a. An object at rest tends to stay at rest until a force acts on it.
    b. An object in motion tends to move at a constant speed until a force acts on it.
    c. The heavier an object is, the more force it takes to change its speed by the same amount.
    d. When an object exerts a force on another object, the second object exerts a force back on the first object.

18. Which of the following words correctly completes this sentence: When the two balls collide, some ____ passes from the first ball to the second ball.

    a. Energy
    b. Length
    c. Time
    d. Weight

19. If the first ball was moving faster, would it have more or less energy than it does now?

    a. More
    b. Less
    c. The same
    d. The ball doesn't have any energy.

Directions: Use the information below and your knowledge of science to answer questions 20 – 23.

A girl finds a caterpillar on a plant and wants to know what kind of butterfly it will become. She puts the caterpillar in an aquarium with a layer of dirt on the bottom and a few sticks for the caterpillar to climb on.

20. What else will she need to put in the jar to keep the caterpillar alive?

    a. Rocks
    b. Grass
    c. A piece of the same kind of plant she found the caterpillar on.
    d. She should be sure to put the jar near a lamp to keep it brightly lit.

21. What is the name of the process when a caterpillar turns into a butterfly?

    a. Evaporation
    b. Metamorphosis
    c. Peristalsis
    d. Respiration

22. The girl's little brother wonders whether the caterpillar will give birth to baby caterpillars. How does the girl know this won't happen?

  a. Caterpillars do not give birth to other caterpillars; they give birth to butterflies.
  b. Caterpillars are not fully grown, and can't reproduce until they become butterflies.
  c. The caterpillar will not have room in the aquarium to reproduce.
  d. The caterpillar must have already reproduced before the girl caught it, and it will not give birth again.

23. Which of these best describes why the caterpillar has a different form from the adult butterfly?

  a. All insects have very different forms as adults; it's in their genetics.
  b. Caterpillars look different from butterflies so the butterflies can tell they're not mature.
  c. The caterpillar has a different lifestyle than the butterfly, so it has a different form appropriate to its needs.
  d. Growing the wings of a butterfly is a very slow process, so it spends time as a caterpillar first to give enough time for the wings to grow.

24. One hazard that may cause a lot of damage to coastal areas is a kind of enormous wave called the *tsunami*. Part of the damage caused by a tsunami is due to the force of the wave hitting structures on the shore. What other effect can a tsunami cause?

  a. Earthquakes
  b. Flooding
  c. Strong winds
  d. Volcanic eruptions

25. Which of the following is most likely to reduce loss of life due to tsunamis?

  a. Building houses close to the shore
  b. Building houses out of brick in threatened areas
  c. Putting strong shutters over windows in threatened areas
  d. Warning systems to alert people when a tsunami is coming

26. What natural phenomenon causes tsunamis?

  a. Solar eclipses
  b. Strong winds
  c. Underwater earthquakes
  d. Unusually high tides

27. One example of a machine that converts one form of energy into another is the engine of a car. The engine uses the stored energy in gasoline. What form of energy does it mainly convert this stored energy into?

  a. Electricity
  b. Light
  c. Motion energy
  d. Sound

28. Which of the following is a form of energy?
   a. Cold
   b. Heat
   c. Speed
   d. Weight

29. Which of the following organs is *not* used to sense things about the outside world?
   a. Ear
   b. Eye
   c. Nose
   d. Stomach

30. Some animals living in caves do not have eyes. What is the best explanation for this?
   a. They don't need eyes because the cave is dark, so they wouldn't be able to see anyway.
   b. Their ancestors' eyes were damaged from radiation in the caves.
   c. Animals living in caves suffer from inbreeding and mutations.
   d. Other animals such as spiders have many eyes, so some have to have no eyes to average things out.

31. What organ in the human body is responsible for the sense of touch?
   a. Eye
   b. Skin
   c. Heart
   d. Tongue

32. Though we say that we use our eyes to see, the eye isn't the only organ involved in vision. What other organ plays a part?
   a. The brain, which processes the information from the eyes
   b. The lungs, which sense qualities in the air that affect what we see
   c. The skin, which detects light coming from other directions
   d. The spleen, which filters the light entering the eyes to help us see different colors

33. The information an animal gets from its senses is one factor that influences its behavior, but an animal's behavior may also depend on its past experiences. What allows animals to learn from the past?
   a. Memory
   b. Evolution
   c. Hormones
   d. Umami

34. Which of the following is a renewable energy source?
   a. Coal
   b. Nuclear power
   c. Oil
   d. Sunlight

Social Studies

Social studies classes cover many different topics. They include learning where people live, how they get along with each other, and how they organize their governments. Along with these subjects, students also learn about history, law, money, and religion, and how they have helped make different people groups what they are today. These social studies questions cover these topics and more, and will help you get more out of your classes.

1. What are the first 10 amendments to the US Constitution called?

    a. Preamble
    b. Articles of Confederation
    c. Declaratory Act
    d. Bill of Rights

2. What is the body of land that forms at the mouth of a river is called?

    a. Delta
    b. Strait
    c. Tongue
    d. Estuary

3. According to the 22nd Amendment, how many consecutive terms may a president serve?

    a. 1
    b. 2
    c. 3
    d. 4

4. Which president sent Lewis and Clark to explore the Louisiana Territory?

    a. John Adams
    b. Thomas Jefferson
    c. James Monroe
    d. William McKinley

5. Which of the following is a type of economic system in which private businesses conduct private transactions through the exchange of goods and services?

    a. Social economy
    b. Market economy
    c. Sales economy
    d. Circular economy

6. Which of the following is the type of government in which all citizens have an equal voice in choosing leaders and making laws?

    a. Monarchy
    b. Oligarchy
    c. Plutocracy
    d. Democracy

7. Which ocean sits on the East Coast of the United States?

   a. Atlantic
   b. Antarctic
   c. Indian
   d. Pacific

8. Which Native American woman accompanied Lewis and Clark on their journey through the Louisiana Purchase?

   a. Shoshone
   b. Pocahontas
   c. Sacagawea
   d. Tecumseh

9. Jamison makes a fixed amount of money each month, and he has a number of bills to pay. To make sure he can pay his bills, Jamison organizes and categorizes his spending. What is Jamison doing?

   a. Making a budget
   b. Creating a savings account
   c. Getting into debt
   d. Starting a business

10. Which of the following could describe a capital resource?

   a. Endangered fish in an estuary
   b. Skilled workers in a plant
   c. River connected to a hydroelectric dam
   d. Electric drill used to build a house

11. In which of the following cases is Lana buying a service instead of a good?

   a. On Saturday, she bought a new pair of shoes from the department store.
   b. Later that afternoon, she went to the salon to get a haircut.
   c. On Sunday, she bought a newspaper from the vendor on the street corner.
   d. She picked up a coffee and a muffin from the local shop on Sunday afternoon.

12. Which of the following presidents delivered the Gettysburg Address?

   a. William Howard Taft
   b. Franklin Delano Roosevelt
   c. Abraham Lincoln
   d. John Adams

13. Which of the following is a major part of determining how businesses operate, what their costs will be, and where they have to make compromises?

   a. Productivity
   b. Benchmarks
   c. Scarcity
   d. Trading

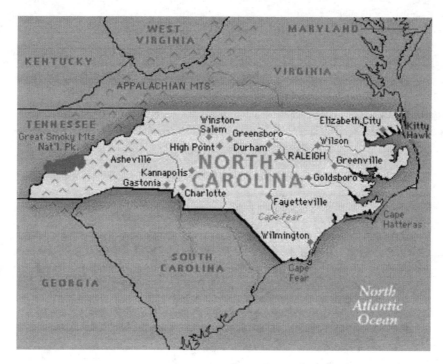

Directions: Use the map above and your knowledge of social studies to answer questions 14 through 17.

14. According to the map, what is the capital of North Carolina?

    a. Raleigh
    b. Greenville
    c. Charlotte
    d. Winston-Salem

15. Which mountains run through North Carolina?

    a. Carolina
    b. Appalachian
    c. Greensboro
    d. Rockies

16. To travel from Kitty Hawk to Asheville, what direction would you go?

    a. North
    b. South
    c. East
    d. West

17. A cape is a high point of land that juts into a body of water and drops off quickly. How many capes, as a type of landform, are indicated on the map of North Carolina?

    a. 2
    b. 3
    c. 4
    d. 5

18. An entrepreneur is starting a new business and is looking carefully at the challenges she will face. Which of the following terms is used to describe similar businesses that the entrepreneur will have to consider to make her own business stand out?

a. Economists
b. Competitors
c. Producers
d. Manufacturers

19. During the Revolutionary War, the Americans who fought on the side of the British were known by what name?

a. Patriots
b. Defenders
c. Loyalists
d. Militiamen

20. The shot heard round the world preceded which Revolutionary War battle?

a. Battles of Lexington and Concord
b. Battle of Fort Washington
c. Battle of Trenton
d. Battle of Saratoga

21. The vice president is part of which branch of government?

a. Legislative
b. Judicial
c. Federal
d. Executive

22. The term *bicameral,* when used to describe the houses of Congress in the United States, indicates that there are how many houses?

a. 2
b. 3
c. 4
d. 6

23. Which president is credited with writing the US Constitution?

a. George Washington
b. James Madison
c. John Tyler
d. Dwight D. Eisenhower

24. What term is used for the part of a map that explains the symbols used on the map?

a. Scheme
b. Scale
c. Compass
d. Legend

25. The term *suffrage* refers to the right that citizens have to do which of the following?

a. Vote
b. Shop
c. Meet
d. Pray

26. Aylmer has an important math test tomorrow, and he knows that he needs to spend some time studying for it. At the same time, his friends have called him to see if he wants to have a pizza party with them. Aylmer has been working very hard on his studies lately, and he would enjoy a break. Which of the following terms reflects the choice that Aylmer has to make?

a. Scarcity of resources
b. Opportunity cost
c. Division of labor
d. Investment opportunity

27. On a map, what are the imaginary lines that run from east to west?

a. Latitude
b. Longitude
c. Meridian
d. Standards

28. Four of the Great Lakes are as follows: Lake Superior, Lake Michigan, Lake Ontario, and Lake Erie. What is the fifth Great Lake?

a. Lake Ohio
b. Lake Minnewanka
c. Lake Huron
d. Lake Niagara

29. The Supreme Court is part of which branch of government?

a. Legislative
b. Judicial
c. Federal
d. Executive

30. How many justices sit on the Supreme Court?

a. 5
b. 7
c. 9
d. 12

31. What is the imaginary line that divides the Northern Hemisphere from the Southern Hemisphere?

a. Prime Meridian
b. Tropic of Cancer
c. Tropic of Capricorn
d. Equator

32. Prior to the American Revolution, in which war did the Americans fight alongside the British?

   a. French and Indian War
   b. Thirty Years' War
   c. Civil War
   d. Wars of the Three Kingdoms

33. Approximately what percentage of the Earth is composed of water?

   a. 35 percent
   b. 50 percent
   c. 70 percent
   d. 85 percent

34. Which conflict occurred shortly after the American Revolution and as a result of a financial depression that left many new Americans struggling to pay debts?

   a. Shays' Rebellion
   b. Northwest Indian War
   c. Whiskey Rebellion
   d. War of 1812

Vocabulary

Did you know the average American adult knows the meaning of over 20,000 words? That's a lot! However, you already know the meanings of thousands of words yourself, and you're learning more all the time. There's a word for the complete set of words you know; it's called your vocabulary.

It's important to build your vocabulary for several reasons. One way a larger vocabulary will help you is by making it easier to do well in school. The more words you know, the easier it will be to learn new things. The same will be true when you get to high school and college. When you start working for a living, having a large vocabulary will help you do well on the job. The following exercise will help you improve your vocabulary.

For each sentence, choose the answer that is the closest in meaning to the word in italics.

1. It was very chilly in the *auditorium*.
   a. waiting room of a doctor's office
   b. shady area under a tree
   c. large room for public meetings
   d. a car with a top that rolls down

2. What do you *suggest*?
   a. enjoy
   b. recommend
   c. dislike
   d. deny

3. It's *fortunate* for her.
   a. lucky
   b. terrible
   c. something that will make one late
   d. something that will confuse someone

4. The *pleasure* is all mine, sir.
   a. money
   b. enjoyment
   c. a tasty dessert
   d. material made from animal skin

5. Compared to her classmates, my sister is very *slender*.
   a. pretty
   b. thin
   c. quiet
   d. smart

6. I *seldom* see him at school.
   a. not very often
   b. very often
   c. early in the morning
   d. late in the afternoon

7. Your brother seems very *mature*.

    a. angry
    b. unfriendly
    c. grown up
    d. not artificial

8. The puppy brought out the *compassion* in Mrs. Jones.

    a. terrible behavior
    b. sleepiness
    c. sympathy
    d. anger

9. I *admire* people like that.

    a. can't stand
    b. know all about
    c. work with
    d. look up to

10. That would be *superb*.

    a. excellent
    b. okay
    c. wrong
    d. silly

11. What do you hope to *accomplish* there?

    a. study
    b. achieve
    c. see
    d. build

12. The line on the page is *vertical*.

    a. straight
    b. going across
    c. going up and down
    d. crooked

13. *Curiosity* got the better of me.

    a. food poisoning
    b. desire to learn
    c. sense of humor
    d. confusion

14. The *lecture* will start soon.

    a. educational talk
    b. sports event
    c. TV show
    d. contest decided by votes

15. He gently corrected his *pupil*.

a. teacher
b. teammate
c. student
d. friend

16. *Agriculture* is something that concerns everyone.

a. farming
b. opera
c. health and fitness
d. being good at math

17. The *population* is growing.

a. large flowering plant
b. number of people in an area
c. group of dark clouds
d. college or university

18. I didn't *recognize* her.

a. go on a date with
b. loan money to
c. identify or remember
d. argue with

19. Billy, please *assist* Cindy.

a. quiet down
b. leave alone
c. show to her seat
d. help

20. The plate glass window was *massive*.

a. huge
b. tiny
c. extremely dirty
d. spotless

21. *United* we stand.

a. here
b. on top
c. underneath
d. together

22. What is the exact *quantity*?

a. number
b. color
c. name
d. length

23. **That was quite a *dispute*.**
    a. sudden loud noise
    b. argument
    c. flashy set of clothes
    d. expensive car

24. **A *severe* storm is headed our way.**
    a. snow
    b. thunder
    c. very bad
    d. not very bad

25. **Heather's *response* made things worse.**
    a. attitude
    b. bad cough
    c. high fever
    d. answer

26. **His story is *fiction*.**
    a. true
    b. false
    c. funny
    d. sad

27. **List your activities by *priority*.**
    a. time of day
    b. enjoyment
    c. importance
    d. how long something takes

28. **Emotions can cause problems in life.**
    a. feelings
    b. waves
    c. movements
    d. actions

29. **We took *drastic* steps to solve the problem.**
    a. very few
    b. several
    c. quick
    d. extreme

30. **We must *tolerate* the noise from the playground.**
    a. drown out
    b. put up with
    c. put a stop to
    d. complain about

31. I know nothing about this *region*.

    a. part of a city, state, or country
    b. system of beliefs about God
    c. very rare disease
    d. person who holds a government office

32. I saw your *former* teacher at the mall today.

    a. new
    b. very good
    c. previous
    d. very tall

33. We didn't make much *progress* today.

    a. money or wealth
    b. news or publicity
    c. forward movement
    d. noisy activity

34. We must *reduce* this fraction.

    a. make bigger
    b. add together
    c. make smaller
    d. make a copy of

Spelling

You should always be striving to improve your spelling skills, because poor spelling not only leads to lower grades, it also makes a bad impression on others. Whether you're writing a short essay for school, or applying for a job, you will be much more successful in life if your writing demonstrates good spelling skills. Fortunately, with regular practice, anyone can become a good speller.

Spelling Exercise

Each question contains four words for you to consider. If one of them is misspelled, circle it. If they are all spelled correctly, circle NO MISTAKES.

#					
1.	wrapped	pray	drink	stomak	NO MISTAKES
2.	rubbing	chaptar	copied	modern	NO MISTAKES
3.	toona	fever	planning	prison	NO MISTAKES
4.	throo	depend	sickness	everything	NO MISTAKES
5.	cities	happen	voyce	glass	NO MISTAKES
6.	charge	mezzure	tiny	little	NO MISTAKES
7.	spare	ture	pepper	good	NO MISTAKES
8.	crooked	tail	gest	stood	NO MISTAKES
9.	emptied	brite	put	waste	NO MISTAKES
10.	library	struck	ring	moon	NO MISTAKES
11.	fifty	speed	lazzy	common	NO MISTAKES
12.	crust	meat	reach	visit	NO MISTAKES
13.	juice	beggur	pull	bottle	NO MISTAKES
14.	guide	bush	rhythm	dere	NO MISTAKES
15.	shokk	kindness	fasten	hour	NO MISTAKES
16.	large	inside	harbor	ansure	NO MISTAKES
17.	wonder	tipe	point	sugar	NO MISTAKES
18.	receive	fireplace	pritty	suit	NO MISTAKES
19.	event	roste	happen	brush	NO MISTAKES
20.	lonely	house	alarm	thirty	NO MISTAKES
21.	against	wood	human	pillow	NO MISTAKES
22.	unhappy	neither	bottom	return	NO MISTAKES
23.	noisier	another	bilt	battle	NO MISTAKES
24.	pilot	safety	serch	style	NO MISTAKES
25.	heart	leson	moment	learn	NO MISTAKES
26.	dizzy	bizzy	eight	guess	NO MISTAKES
27.	banana	turkey	uncle	pruve	NO MISTAKES

Capitalization

Proper capitalization is very important in writing. Knowing which words to capitalize, and when, is one of the skills every person should possess. Improper capitalization can cause a reader to think the writer isn't very smart. Many people won't pay any attention to writing that contains capitalization errors. In high school and college, making capitalization mistakes on the papers you will need to write may result in a failing grade. So it's vital that you learn how to use proper capitalization.

Read each numbered item, and then decide if it's capitalized correctly, or incorrectly. If it's capitalized incorrectly, choose the answer which contains the mistake. If it's capitalized correctly, choose NO MISTAKES. Sentences may contain words that aren't capitalized that should be, or words that are capitalized that shouldn't be, or both.

1. My mom said uncle Bob will pick up a book about snakes for me to read.

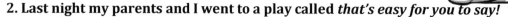

    a. My mom said uncle Bob
    b. will pick up a book about snakes
    c. for me to read.
    d. NO MISTAKES

2. Last night my parents and I went to a play called *that's easy for you to say!*

    a. Last night my parents and I
    b. went to a play called
    c. that's easy for you to say!
    d. NO MISTAKES

3. Christmas falls on the same day every year – december 25th.

    a. Christmas falls on
    b. the same day every year
    c. – december 25th.
    D. NO MISTAKES

4. We visited my cousins in Kansas city, Missouri last year for vacation.

    a. We visited my cousins
    b. in Kansas city, Missouri
    c. last year for vacation.
    d. NO MISTAKES

5. I would like to make an appointment on Friday with doctor Jones.

    a. I would like to make
    b. an appointment on Friday
    c. with doctor Jones.
    d. NO MISTAKES

6. "watch the ball, Frank!" yelled Coach Johnson from the bench.

    a. "watch the ball, Frank!"
    b. yelled Coach Johnson
    c. from the bench.
    d. NO MISTAKES

7. After the game, a reporter from the Newspaper interviewed Coach Johnson.

- a. After the game, a reporter
- b. from the Newspaper
- c. interviewed Coach Johnson.
- d. NO MISTAKES

8. We stopped at Yellowstone National park on the way to Grampa's house.

- a. We stopped at
- b. Yellowstone National park
- c. on the way to Grampa's house.
- d. NO MISTAKES

9. Dr. Bramley is Chairman of the Department of Astronomy.

- a. Dr. Bramley
- b. is Chairman of
- c. the Department of Astronomy.
- d. NO MISTAKES

10. Muslims believe in Allah and follow the teachings of the koran.

- a. Muslims believe in Allah
- b. and follow the teachings
- c. of the koran.
- d. NO MISTAKES

11. Bill Gates is the Founder of the company called Microsoft.

- a. Bill Gates is
- b. the Founder of
- c. the company called Microsoft.
- d. NO MISTAKES

12. We learned about world war II in class today.

- a. We learned about
- b. world war II
- c. in class today.
- d. NO MISTAKES

13. The holidays of Christmas and New year's Day are a week apart.

- a. The holidays of Christmas
- b. and New year's Day are
- c. a week apart.
- d. NO MISTAKES

14. Next sunday my baby brother is getting baptized.

- a. Next sunday
- b. my baby brother
- c. is getting baptized.
- d. NO MISTAKES

15. **In my opinion, no salad is complete without italian dressing.**

    a. In my opinion,
    b. no salad is complete
    c. without italian dressing.
    d. NO MISTAKES

16. **One of the greatest painters in the History of Italy was Michelango.**

    a. One of the greatest painters
    b. in the History of Italy
    c. was Michelango.
    d. NO MISTAKES

17. **We went to the museum of science and industry in Chicago, Illinois.**

    a. We went to
    b. the museum of science and industry
    c. in Chicago, Illinois.
    d. NO MISTAKES

18. **"Class, we will have a quiz on Friday," said mrs. van buren.**

    a. "Class, we will have
    b. a quiz on Friday,"
    c. said Mrs. Van buren.
    d. NO MISTAKES

19. **"My german shepherd's name shall be Charlie," said Heather.**

    a. "My german shepherd's name
    b. shall be Charlie,"
    c. said Heather.
    d. NO MISTAKES

20. **Sara said, "Mom, can we go visit Grandma this weekend?"**

    a. Sara said,
    b. "Mom, can we go visit
    c. Grandma this weekend?"
    d. NO MISTAKES

21. **My friend in England is a distant relative of king George III.**

    a. My friend in England
    b. is a distant relative
    c. of king George III.
    d. NO MISTAKES

22. **Our teacher said that jupiter and saturn are the two biggest planets.**

    a. Our teacher said that
    b. jupiter and saturn are
    c. the two biggest planets.
    d. NO MISTAKES

Punctuation

Punctuation is one of the things that make reading understandable and enjoyable. Thousands of years ago punctuation didn't exist. When someone wrote something they wrote it without periods, commas, question marks, or any other punctuation at all. Can you imagine trying to read something that didn't have any punctuation? It would be like reading a sentence that was several pages long. It would be very confusing. That's why punctuation was created -- to help make it easier to understand what a writer was trying to say. Of course, punctuation doesn't help a reader understand written material if the writer doesn't know how to use it. This exercise will help you discover if you know how to punctuate properly.

The text in each question may contain a punctuation error. If there is an error, select the answer choice which contains the error. If there is no error, select NO MISTAKES.

1. Exasperated we finally found the ball in a place you would never guess.
- a. Exasperated we finally found
- b. the ball in a place
- c. you would never guess.
- d. NO MISTAKES

2. The big game the one I've been telling you about all week – starts in exactly one hour.
- a. The big game the one I've been
- b. telling you about all week – starts
- c. in exactly one hour.
- d. NO MISTAKES

3. As the crowd cheered him on, Rico bent his knees, swung for the fences and struck out.
- a. As the crowd cheered him on,
- b. Rico bent his knees, swung for the fences
- c. and struck out.
- d. NO MISTAKES

4. Our new gym teacher Mr. Ronson told us he was born in England.
- a. Our new gym
- b. teacher Mr. Ronson
- c. told us he was born in England.
- d. NO MISTAKES

5. We can either go to the park or we can stay here and play games.
- a. We can either go to
- b. the park or we can
- c. stay here and play games.
- d. NO MISTAKES

6. Sadly, the team lost it's final game of the season.
- a. Sadly, the team
- b. lost it's final game
- c. of the season.
- d. NO MISTAKES

7. James was disappointed he had hoped to pass the test.

    a. James was disappointed
    b. he had hoped to
    c. pass the test.
    d. NO MISTAKES

8. Only three students got an A on the exam, Sam, Wilma, and Pedro.

    a. Only three students got
    b. an A on the exam,
    c. Sam, Wilma, and Pedro.
    d. NO MISTAKES

9. While getting ready I noticed it had begun to rain.

    a. While getting ready
    b. I noticed it had
    c. begun to rain.
    d. NO MISTAKES

10. Sam Wilma and Pedro all got an A on the math test today.

    a. Sam Wilma and Pedro
    b. all got an A on
    c. the math test today.
    d. NO MISTAKES

11. I borrowed some books from the library Billy wants to come over tonight.

    a. I borrowed some books from
    b. the library Billy wants to
    c. come over tonight.
    d. NO MISTAKES

12. It's half past five Grandma and Grandpa should be here any minute.

    a. It's half past five
    b. Grandma and Grandpa should
    c. be here any minute.
    d. NO MISTAKES

13. Susie, Mom said, "I think it's time for you to go to bed."

    a. Susie, Mom said,
    b. "I think it's time for
    c. you to go to bed."
    d. NO MISTAKES

14. Yes Mom I have made my bed and taken out the trash.

    a. Yes Mom I have
    b. made my bed and
    c. taken out the trash.
    d. NO MISTAKES

15. Because we're going on a field trip we have to arrive at school early.

    a.   Because we're going on
    b.   a field trip we have to
    c.   arrive at school early.
    d.   NO MISTAKES

16. Class, we will all meet at the bus at 730 tomorrow morning.

    a.   Class, we will all
    b.   meet at the bus at
    c.   730 tomorrow morning.
    d.   NO MISTAKES

17. Actually, this is Tony's classroom Tammy's classroom is down the hall.

    a.   Actually, this is Tony's
    b.   classroom Tammy's classroom
    c.   is down the hall.
    d.   NO MISTAKES

18. My favorite baseball player Babe Ruth played about 100 years ago.

    a.   My favorite baseball
    b.   player Babe Ruth played
    c.   about 100 years ago.
    d.   NO MISTAKES

19. Our teacher said I don't think so when we asked if there would be a test.

    a.   Our teacher said
    b.   I don't think so when we asked
    c.   if there would be a test.
    d.   NO MISTAKES

20. We should never lose sight of whats really important.

    a.   We should never
    b.   lose sight of
    c.   whats really important.
    d.   NO MISTAKES

21. "Yes, kids, its true that the test has been canceled," said Mr. Johnson.

    a.   "Yes, kids, its true that
    b.   the test has been canceled,"
    c.   said Mr. Johnson.
    d.   NO MISTAKES

22. My dad works for the Federal Bureau of Investigation FBI.

    a.   My dad works
    b.   for the Federal
    c.   Bureau of Investigation FBI.
    d.   NO MISTAKES

Practice Test Answers and Explanations

Reading

1. B: The Land of Oz. The Witch of the North refers to "this Land of Oz" and the great desert that surrounds it. The exact quote is: "'The North is my home,' said the old lady, 'and at its edge is the same great desert that surrounds *this Land of Oz*. I'm afraid, my dear, you will have to live with us.'"

2. A: Return to her aunt and uncle. Dorothy says she wants to return to her aunt and uncle because they will be worried about her. She asks the Munchkins and the Witch of the North to help her. The passage states: "Dorothy carried the shoes into the house and placed them on the table. Then she came out again to the Munchkins and said: '*I am anxious to get back to my aunt and uncle*, for I am sure they will worry about me. Can you help me find my way?'"

3. D: Sad. Dorothy feels anxious and sad about her situation. Her emotions are evident when she begins to cry: "*Dorothy began to sob* at this, for she felt lonely among all these strange people. Her tears seemed to grieve the kind-hearted Munchkins, for they immediately took out their handkerchiefs and began to weep also."

4. B: She suggests that Dorothy ask the Wizard of Oz for help and gives Dorothy a kiss for protection. The Witch of the North says: "Then you must go to the City of Emeralds. Perhaps Oz will help you." At the end of the passage she gives Dorothy a kiss: "'No, I cannot do that,' she replied, 'but I will give you my kiss, and no one will dare injure a person who has been kissed by the Witch of the North.' She came close to Dorothy and kissed her gently on the forehead. Where her lips touched the girl, they left a round, shining mark, as Dorothy found out soon after."

5. C: To ask the Wizard of Oz for help. The Witch of the North says: "Then you must go to the City of Emeralds. Perhaps Oz will help you." Dorothy asks, "How can I get there?" The Witch of the North replies, "You must walk. It is a long journey, through a country that is sometimes pleasant and sometimes dark and terrible. However, I will use all the magic arts I know of to keep you from harm."

6. A: Cry. Students should use context clues to determine that Dorothy's tears cause the Munchkins to create their own tears.

7. B: Nice. Students should use context clues to determine that the word pleasant means the opposite of "dark and terrible."

8. B: "How do I find the City of Emeralds?" Dorothy asked the Witch of the North. Before Dorothy can begin her journey, she needs to know how to find the City of Emeralds. Choices A and C tell what might happen later in Dorothy's journey. Choice D is a question Dorothy might ask, but it is not necessary to beginning her journey.

9. D: "Stay right beside me, Toto," said Dorothy nervously to her little black dog. This sentence best conveys Dorothy's feelings of anxiety at being in a strange land and beginning what is sure to be a difficult journey. The other sentence choices are statements of fact (Choice C), opinion (Choice B), or a practical statement that does not express any particular emotion (Choice A).

10. A: Dorothy followed the yellow brick road through the green countryside dotted with little blue houses. This is the only sentence choice that describes the setting of the story for the reader. The other sentence choices describe what Dorothy does (Choice B) and how she feels (Choices C and D).

11. C: Finally, Dorothy came upon a shady tree and sat down under its leaves to rest. Students should use the transition word "finally" to signal that this event happens after Dorothy has been walking for a long time. The other sentence choices indicate events that might happen before Dorothy started her walk (Choices B and D) or during her walk (Choice A).

12. B: Dorothy was tired after her long walk and soon fell asleep. This is the only sentence choice that follows naturally from the previous events in the paragraph. The other sentence choices describe events that might have occurred earlier (Choices A and C) and how Dorothy and Toto feel (Choice D).

13. B: How to set up an aquarium. The main idea of this article is the beginning basics of setting up an aquarium.

14. A: Tropical freshwater species. The article states: "Tropical freshwater species are the easiest fish to keep because their needs change based on their surroundings and the resources they have available. They are able to adapt to living in different environments."

15. D: Choose your fish. The article states: "Choose your fish first. This will tell you what type of tank, water, and plants you need."

16. C: Tropical freshwater species. The article states: "Some tropical freshwater fish are the rosy barb, angelfish, and x-ray fish."

17. B: To change in order to fit in. The preceding sentence and this sentence together give the reader the context needed to understand the word: "Tropical freshwater species are the easiest fish to keep because their needs change based on their surroundings and the resources they have available. They are able to adapt to living in different environments."

18. C: If my fish usually live in schools, how many of that kind do I need? This answer choice asks the author to expand on information given in the article: "If the type of fish you chose normally live in schools, or groups, that means they are social fish. You will need to buy more than one of that kind to keep your fish from being lonely." The other answer choices are off topic (Choice A) or ask for information about fish that is not directly related to setting up an aquarium (Choices B and D).

19. B: Butterflies are interesting and beautiful insects. This is the best answer choice because it is a general statement that tells what the paragraph will be about. The other answer choices are detail sentences that give additional information about butterflies.

20. A: A butterfly is an insect with a thin body and four wings. Choice A is the definition of a butterfly. It gives more information about what a butterfly is than the definition in Choice C. Choices B and D are details about butterflies, not definitions.

21. D: Another example of a butterfly that is poisonous to eat is a Monarch butterfly. This is the best sentence to follow the sentence given: A Pipevine Swallowtail butterfly is poisonous to eat. Choice A is a description of butterflies, Choice B repeats information already in the given sentence, and Choice C gives information about the butterfly's life cycle.

22. C: During a process called metamorphosis, a caterpillar changes into a chrysalis and then an adult butterfly. This sentence gives the most information about the life cycle of a butterfly. Choice A gives some information about the butterfly's life cycle, but the information is not as complete as it is in Choice C. Choices B and D give other information about butterflies that is not directly related to their life cycle.

23. B: A butterfly drinks flower nectar through a tube in its mouth called a proboscis. Choice B gives the most complete information about a butterfly's eating habits. Choices A and C give information about a butterfly's eating habits, but not as much information as Choice B. Choice D gives information that is unrelated to a butterfly's eating habits.

24. C: Butterflies are insects that begin life as caterpillars, change through metamorphosis, and eat flower nectar through a tube called a proboscis. This is the only answer choice that provides a summary of information about butterflies.

25. D: Nonfiction (true) biography. This is the best choice for the most information about Abraham Lincoln's life. A dictionary (Choice A) would tell you who Abraham Lincoln was, but it would not give you detailed information about his life. A thesaurus (Choice B) is a book of synonyms and antonyms and would not give you any information about Abraham Lincoln. A fiction (made up) short story (Choice C) might be about Abraham Lincoln, but since it is fiction (made up), you could not be sure that the information was true.

26. B: Childhood, Adulthood, Greatest Accomplishments. This answer choice includes three important categories of information about Abraham Lincoln: his childhood, his adulthood, and his accomplishments as president. Choice A has childhood and adulthood, but also includes favorite foods, which is not an important category. Choice C includes only categories from Abraham Lincoln's early life. Choice D includes two categories of information that may be interesting but are not important: favorite foods and hobbies.

27. A: Abraham Lincoln was born on February 12, 1809. This is the only answer choice that includes information from Abraham Lincoln's childhood. All of the other answer choices have information about Abraham Lincoln's adulthood.

28. D: Timeline of events in Abraham Lincoln's life. Although all of the other choices would give information about Abraham Lincoln, a timeline is the best choice for a biography because it would show the important events across the entire span of Lincoln's life.

29. C: stammered nervously. The sentences should read: "I don't like being the center of attention. I can't get up and speak in front of all of those people," Peter stammered nervously. The context of the sentence indicates that Peter is nervous.

30. B: which. The sentence should read: The movie, which was about a baseball player, started late. The part of the sentence set off by commas "_____ was about a baseball player" is a nonrestrictive relative clause. The sentence can stand on its own without this clause: The movie started late. If the sentence could not stand on its own, the commas would be removed and the word "that" would be the correct choice.

31. B: will be. The sentence should read: I will be taking the bus to school tomorrow. Based on the context of the sentence, which indicates a time in the future, the correct answer is the future progressive tense: "will be taking."

32. D: field, Friday. The sentence should read: Our class is taking a field trip on Friday. Days of the week are capitalized. Field is not capitalized unless it is at the beginning of a sentence.

33. B: too, to. The sentence should read: The bookshelf was too high for Daniel to reach.

34. A: vacation, January. The sentence should read: We are going on our family vacation in January.

35. A: "May I go to the movies with John tomorrow?" Sam asked his mom. Speech belongs inside quotation marks. If the speech is a question, the question mark belongs inside the quotation marks, as shown in Choice A. The part of the sentence identifying the speaker belongs outside of the quotation marks.

36. C: Molly, watch out for the runaway train! The sentence is an exclamation, a warning to keep away from the runaway train. This calls for an exclamation point.

37. D: Maria wanted to give a party for her mom, and she wanted it to be a surprise. A comma is used before the coordinating conjunction "and" in this compound sentence.

38. B: Enemy. The word ally means a friend or someone who is with you for a common purpose. Enemy is the opposite of ally.

39. C: Spoke strongly against. The context of the sentence should be used to determine the meaning of the word protested.

40. D: Brag about your accomplishments. The word boast means to brag about your accomplishments or talk about yourself with pride.

41. B: Friends bring color and happiness into our lives. Friends are the flowers in the garden of life. This is a metaphor saying that life is a garden and friends are the flowers in that garden. Flowers bring color, beauty, and happiness to everyone who sees them. In the same way, friends bring color, beauty, and happiness into our lives.

42. A: Always think about your actions before doing anything. "Look before you leap" means stop and think before you take action, considering the consequences of your decisions in advance.

Written Expression

1. Whoever

2. where

3. whom

4. when

5. I am riding my bike.

6. I am playing chess.

7. We were studying for the test because we didn't want to fail.

8. We were reading quietly when the teacher announced a surprise quiz.

9. will be playing

10. am going to be studying

11. can

12. must

13. D: the big old yellow bus

14. C: the hilarious old Canadian clown

15. by

16. regarding

17. after lunch – ADV

18. Except for Lawanda – ADJ

19. C

20. F

21. R

22. C

23. principal

24. their

25. I arrive at school every day at 8 AM. | I arrive at school every weekday at 8 AM.

26. If it starts raining, we'll go inside.

27. A: accomplice

28. D: frigid

29. Trent turns into a bulldozer | Trent turns into a strong person who runs other players over

30. like a dream come true | it was something I had wanted to do for a long time

31. raining extremely hard

32. go to bed

33. the mice will play

34. before they hatch

35. hideous

36. inferior

37. rare

38. stingy

Mathematics

1. A: If there are 7 pens with 3 cattle, then the total number of cattle is found by $7 \times 3 = 21$, not 20. In the other problems, $8 \times 3 = 24, 3 \times 8 = 24$, and $3 \times 7 = 21$.

2. B: The cost of one eraser is found by dividing the total cost by the number of erasers. Since the cost of the erasers is $4.50, and there are 18 erasers, the expression for the cost of the eraser will be $4.50 ÷ 18 = $0.25. The total cost of one eraser is $0.25

3. C: If Raquel had 36 stamps and divided them into 9 groups, there will be 4 stamps per group because $36 ÷ 9 = 4$. She then adds 2 stamps to each group so that she has 6 stamps per group. Since there are nine groups of six and $9 \times 6 = 54$, she has a total of 54 stamps. If she gives 4 stamps each to 13 friends, she gives away $4 \times 13 = 52$ stamps. This means she has $54 - 52 = 2$ stamps left over.= 13 r 2, so she gave four stamps to each of her 13 friends and had a remainder of 2

4. C: One number is the factor of another if it will divide it with no remainder. Ten is not a factor of twelve because $12 ÷ 10 = 1$ remainder 2. Also, ten is not a factor of twenty-four because $24 ÷ 10 = 2$ remainder 4. Six is not a factor of eighty because $80 ÷ 6 = 13$ remainder 2. The correct answer is sixty, because 4, 6 and 10 all divide it evenly.

5. D: The first figure had 6 sides. The second figure has 11 sides because 5 sides had to be added to make the next figure. This pattern of adding 5 segments continued, so the answers had to be 6, 11, 16, and 21.

6. D: $90 \times 10 = 900$, so 900 is 10 times greater than 90. 800 is 100 times greater than 8, 3000 is 100 times greater than 30, and 70 is only a tenth of 700. Therefore the only answer is D.

7. B: The value of A is 5,032,080; the value of C is 5,320,008; and the value of D is 5,328. B shows 5,320,080 which is the original number.

8. D: The 8 is in the hundreds place, and because the number to the right of 8 is a five, the 8 must round up to a 9. The remaining numbers change to a 0. Therefore the answer is 7,900.

9. B: Adding the ones place, you get 10, so the one carries to the tens place. 1+8+5=14, so the 4 goes in the tens place and the 1 is carried over the hundreds place. 1+4+3=8, so the 8 goes into the hundreds place. The final answer is 840.

$$452$$

$$+388$$

$$840$$

10. C: To subtract the ones column, a 1 has to be borrowed from the tens column, so the 0 becomes 10 and the 5 becomes a 4. $10 - 7 = 3$, so the 3 goes in the ones unit. To subtract the tens column, a 1 needs to be borrowed from the 2 in the hundreds column. That 2 becomes 1 and the 4 in the tens column becomes 14. $14 - 8 = 6$, so the 6 goes in the tens column. Finally the 1 is borrowed from the thousands column so that 1 becomes 0 in the thousands column and the 1 in the hundreds column becomes 11. $11 - 4 = 7$ so the 7 goes in the hundreds place of the answer. The final answer is 763.

$$1250$$

$$\underline{-487}$$

$$763$$

11. A: The formula for the area of a rectangle is Area = length × width. The length is 32 and the width is 14. So,

$$32$$

$$\underline{\times 14}$$

$$128$$

$$\underline{+320}$$

$$448$$

So the area is 448 square units.

12. A: Setting up the multiplication problem into the standard method, $7 \times 7 = 49$, so the 9 gets written into the ones column and a +4 gets written above the tens column. $7 \times 5 + 4 = 39$ so the 9 gets written into the tens column and a +3 gets written above the hundreds column. $7 \times 4 + 3 = 31$, so the 31 is written in the thousands and hundreds place. The final answer is 3199.

$$457$$

$$\underline{\times 7}$$

$$3199$$

13. D: Using long division:

```
        1436 r 5
     6|8621
      -6
       26
      -24
        22
       -18
        41
       -36
         5
```

14. C: The fraction for C is $\frac{3}{8}$ because it is the number of shaded blocks over the number of total blocks. Every other answer reduces to $\frac{3}{5}$.

15. A: $\frac{6}{18}$ reduces to $\frac{1}{3}$ by dividing 6 from the numerator and denominator; $\frac{2}{6}$ also reduces to $\frac{1}{3}$ by dividing 2 from the numerator and denominator; so $\frac{6}{18} = \frac{2}{6}$.

16. A: Rewrite $\frac{2}{3}$ and $\frac{3}{5}$ to have common denominator of 15. For $\frac{2}{3}$, multiply both the numerator and denominator by 5 to see that $\frac{2}{3} = \frac{10}{15}$. For $\frac{3}{5}$, multiply the numerator and denominator by 3 to see that $\frac{3}{5} = \frac{9}{15}$. Comparing $\frac{10}{15}$ and $\frac{9}{15}$, it's simple to see that $\frac{10}{15}$ is larger than $\frac{9}{15}$, because the numerator is larger and the denominator is the same. . $\frac{10}{15} > \frac{9}{15}$, therefore $\frac{2}{3} > \frac{3}{5}$.

17. B: If $\frac{3}{8}$ and $\frac{2}{5}$ are written to have common denominators of 40, their equivalent fractions would be $\frac{3}{8} = \frac{15}{40}$ by multiplying the numerator and denominator by 5; and $\frac{2}{5} = \frac{16}{40}$ by multiplying the numerator and denominator by 8. $\frac{15}{40} < \frac{16}{40}$, therefore $\frac{3}{8} < \frac{2}{5}$.

18. C: The first box is $\frac{9}{16}$ and the second box is $\frac{4}{16}$. The sum of the two boxes is $\frac{9}{16} + \frac{4}{16} = \frac{13}{16}$ because the numerators will add to 13, but the denominator remains common.

19. A: $\frac{8}{8} - \frac{1}{8} - \frac{1}{8} - \frac{1}{8} - \frac{1}{8} = \frac{4}{8}$, not 5/8. $\frac{2}{8} + \frac{2}{8} + \frac{1}{8} = \frac{5}{8}$; $\frac{1}{8} + \frac{1}{8} + \frac{1}{8} + \frac{1}{8} + \frac{1}{8} = \frac{5}{8}$; and $\frac{1}{8} + \frac{2}{8} + \frac{3}{8} + \frac{4}{8} - \frac{5}{8} = \frac{5}{8}$ so it cannot be B, C, or D.

20. B: The whole numbers 4 and 3 add up to 7 and the fractions $\frac{1}{5}$ and $\frac{2}{5}$ add up to $\frac{3}{5}$, so the sum is $7\frac{3}{5}$ by putting the whole number and fraction part together.

21. D: The whole numbers 11 and 8 subtract to 3 and the fractions $\frac{3}{5}$ and $\frac{2}{5}$ subtract to $\frac{1}{5}$. So putting the whole number part and fractional part together, the difference is $3\frac{1}{5}$.

22. C: Reducing a recipe by a specific amount means to subtract the smaller amount, $\frac{2}{3}$, from the larger amount, $2\frac{1}{3}$. The mathematical expression becomes $2\frac{1}{3} - \frac{2}{3} = \frac{7}{3} - \frac{2}{3} = \frac{5}{3} = 1\frac{2}{3}$. Therefore $1\frac{2}{3}$ cup of sugar is needed for the recipe.

23. A: To determine the total length, the length of one pendulum, $\frac{1}{12}$ meter, has to be multiplied by the numbers of pendulums, 5. The mathematical expression becomes $5 \times \frac{1}{12} = \frac{5}{12}$.

24. D: The 4 multiplies only to the numerator of 3, so $4 \times \frac{3}{5} = \frac{12}{5}$. Another way is to rewrite 4 as $\frac{4}{1}$; then $\frac{4}{1} \times \frac{3}{5} = \frac{12}{5}$ because the numerators multiply together and the denominators multiply together.

25. B: There are 4 boxes that show $\frac{8}{25}$ shaded. To find the total amount shaded, multiply the 4 by $\frac{8}{25}$. So the mathematical expression becomes $4 \times \frac{8}{25} = \frac{32}{25}$.

26. C: To determine the total length of rope needed, the length of one rope, $\frac{1}{2}$ meter, needs to be multiplied by the total number of pieces needed, 9. The mathematical expression is $9 \times \frac{1}{2} = \frac{9}{2} = 4\frac{1}{2}$.

27. A: $\frac{7}{10} + \frac{57}{100}$ have a common denominator of 100. $\frac{7}{10} = \frac{70}{100}$ by multiplying the numerator and denominator by 10. Then adding $\frac{70}{100} + \frac{57}{100} = \frac{127}{100}$ by adding only the numerators and keeping the denominator common.

28. A: In $\frac{45}{100}$, the decimal moves from behind the 5 two spaces to the left because of the division by 100. The answer becomes 0.45.

29. B: First compare the tenths spot of the numbers. 2 > 1 therefore 0.24 > 0.18. The numbers after the tenth can be ignored.

30. D: Because there are 1000 meters in a kilometer, we divide the distance in meters by 1000 to find the distance expressed in kilometers. $3490 \div 1000 = 3.49$. The decimal moves three spaces to the left. 3490 meters is the same as 3.49 kilometers.

31. A: Multiply the amount of money you make per day by the number of days in a week to

determine the amount of money you would make in a week, that is $\$40.25 \times 5 = \$201.25$. Then subtract the amount saved from the amount per week to give the spending money per week. That is $\$201.25 - \$20 = \$181.25$.

32. D: To find the perimeter, all of the sides of the rectangle must be added up. There are two sides that are 52 meters in length and two sides that are 18 meters in length. The sum of all four sides is 52+52+18+18 = 140, so the perimeter is 140 meters.

33. D: The two distances must be subtracted to determine how much farther Richard ran than Mary. The expression becomes $\frac{5}{8} - \frac{1}{2} = \frac{5}{8} - \frac{4}{8} = \frac{1}{8}$. Therefore Richard ran $\frac{1}{8}$ mile more than Mary on that day.

34. B: 180 of the $\frac{1}{360}$ th one-degree angles need to be multiplied. The expression becomes $180 \times \frac{1}{360} = \frac{180}{360} = \frac{1}{2}$. Therefore 180° is $\frac{1}{2}$ of the circle.

35. C: The sum of the two non-overlapping angles is 52+41=93. Therefore the measure of $\angle ABC = 93°$.

36. A: Using a protractor, with one ray lined up on the zero, the other ray will point to 45°. Therefore the measure of the angle is 45°.

37. D: $\angle ABC$ is made up of the combination of the two smaller angles, $\angle ABD$ and $\angle DBC$. The measure of the missing angle, $\angle ABD$, is the same as the difference of the large angle and the smaller known angle. To find the measure of the missing angle, we subtract $\angle DBC$ from $\angle ABC$. be subtracted from it. The expression becomes $m\angle ABC = 100° - 22° = 78°$.

38. B: Because the angle is opened up greater than a right angle, and not a straight line, the angle is classified as an obtuse angle.

39. B: Because the four-sided figure has exactly one pair of parallel lines, the quadrilateral is a trapezoid. A rhombus has two pairs of parallel sides, a kite does not have parallel sides, and a pentagon has 5 sides, so it cannot be any of those choices.

40. C: The scalene triangle does not have a line of symmetry. The hexagon has six lines of symmetry, the arrow has one line of symmetry and the curve has one line of symmetry.

Science

1. C: The human eye works by detecting light that reflects off of (or is emitted by) other objects. In order for the eye to detect that light, the light must enter the eye. The white part of the eye (the sclera) is opaque; light can't get through it. The pupil is the hole through which the light enters the eye; it looks black because very little of the light that enters through the pupil is reflected back out of it. (Although your pupil lets light through, it doesn't let through air or other materials; it's covered by a transparent layer called the cornea.)

2. B: The *cornea* is the transparent front part of the eye. The iris is the colored ring surrounding the pupil, and the retina lines the inner rear surface of the eye. The cochlea is not a part of the eye at all, but the ear.

3. B: We see objects because either they emit light that enters our eye, or they reflect light that enters our eye. Although it's true that glass doesn't emit light, neither does metal, so that doesn't explain why the glass can't be seen but the metal can. The best explanation is choice B, that the glass does not reflect light—light passes right through it. As for choices C and D, although there are other "kinds" of light outside the visible range, such as ultraviolet and infrared, they don't in any way "cancel" visible light.

4. C: To test the theory, it would be best to try to repeat the circumstances; that is, if you think the plants are responsible for changing the soil, introduce the plants into a sample of unchanged soil and see whether and how the plants affect it. The procedures described in choices A and B may tell you more about the plants, but they would not directly show anything about the plants' effect on the soil.

5. D: As water from rainfall flows across the ground, either through rivers and streams or along the ground, it often carries soil and sediment from one place to another. *Evaporation* is something that happens to water and other liquids, not to soil, and *continental drift* is a very slow process that involves entire continents and will not be responsible for the local movement of soil. The same goes for *plate tectonics*, which is a term for the general phenomenon of the movement of the Earth's crust and includes continental drift.

6. A: *Erosion* is the breakdown of rock into soil and the movement of soil from place to place, caused by wind, water, ice, and other phenomena. *Geology* is the study of minerals and the Earth, *glaciation* is the formation of glaciers (large sheets of ice), and *metamorphosis* can refer to various processes of change, including a change in a rock due to high pressure or temperature.

7. A: The height of a wave is called its *amplitude*. The *frequency* of a wave is the number of waves that pass by a given point in a particular amount of time. *Intensity* and *power* have various meanings in physics, but none of them relates directly to the height of a wave.

8. D: Aside from *amplitude* (height), another important characteristic of waves is their *wavelength*, the distance between two peaks. *Depth* and *intensity* are not well-defined characteristics of waves distinct from their amplitudes.

9. A: Although the wave itself may move horizontally, each particular bit of water within the wave is just moving up and down; it does not move sideways along with the wave. The same will apply for the toothpicks that are floating in the water. The process is similar to people doing the "wave" in a stadium—the wave moves around the stadium, but each individual person is only moving up and down.

10. D: As described in the text, phloem and xylem carry water and chemicals between different parts of the plant, just like the veins and arteries carry water and chemicals between different parts of the human body.

11. B: The main purpose of the flower in a plant is in reproduction; the flower attracts pollinators such as bees that carry the pollen from one flower to another. If two otherwise similar plants develop flowers with a very different appearance, it's possible they did so to attract different pollinators.

12. C: The main purpose of thorns in a plant is defensive, to fend off herbivores that would otherwise feed on it. A plant with large thorns, therefore, is likely to have grown in an area with large herbivores it would have had to defend against.

13. D: One way the botanist could possibly figure out what the bulbs do is to see what happens differently to the plants with the bulbs removed; this would suggest what purpose the bulbs are serving in a healthy plant. None of the other options would be as effective: just because a feature on another plant looks similar doesn't mean it serves a similar purpose; watching the plants grow in another area is unlikely to show what the bulbs do, and the bulbs may not do anything when severed from the plants.

14. B: The map shows no earthquakes in Australia itself, although it does show a few in the ocean not far from the Australian shore. All the other continents listed have several earthquakes shown; next to Australia, the continent with the fewest earthquakes is South America, in which only two earthquakes occurred.

15. D: Earthquakes tend to occur along the edges of continental plates; an earthquake happens as two plates move past or rub against each other. Volcanoes also occur at the edges of continental plates as magma slips between the continental plates. On the other hand, canyons often occur from erosion by rivers and may readily exist in the middle of a plate. Cyclones and thunderstorms do not have any particular reason to occur more frequently at the edge of a continental plate.

16. D: An earthquake on the ocean floor may cause a large wave in the ocean, which remains low (but broad) in the deep ocean but piles up on itself and grows to a very large height as it approaches the shore. Such a wave is known as a *tsunami*, or popularly as a tidal wave (even though it has nothing to do with the tide). *Hurricanes* and *monsoons* are weather phenomena that have no connection to earthquakes, and *eclipses* are caused by the relative position of the Sun and the Moon and also have no relation to earthquakes.

17. C: All of those statements are true—in fact, they're paraphrases of Newton's laws of motion, some of the most basic laws of classical mechanics. However, not all of them are shown by this demonstration. The fact that the second ball doesn't move until the first ball hits it supports the statement in choice A; the fact that the first ball moves at a constant speed until it hits the second (as seen by the fact that it has the same spacing in successive frames) supports the statement in choice B. The fact that the first ball slows down as it hits the second ball suggests that there is some force acting on it to the left, and it supports choice D. However, because we know nothing about the weights of the balls, nothing in the observation clearly supports choice C.

18. A: Energy can be transferred from one object to another by collisions. This is not true of any of the quantities in the other choices. Not all of the energy lost by the first ball goes into the second ball; some also goes into the air, creating heat and sound.

19. A: The faster an object is moving, the more energy it has.

20. C: The caterpillar will need food, and it is likely that the same kind of plant that the girl found the caterpillar on is the kind that it eats. A caterpillar can't necessarily eat every kind of plant, so grass won't necessarily help, and rocks and light aren't needed for a caterpillar's development. (Caterpillars also don't need to be given water; they get the moisture they need from the plants they eat.)

21. B: When a caterpillar turns into a butterfly, the process is called *metamorphosis*. (The same term applies to other times that organisms undergo significant changes between their juvenile and adult forms, such as a tadpole turning into a frog.) *Evaporation* is when a liquid changes into a gas (such as when a puddle of water dries up), *peristalsis* is the process by which your digestive tract pushes food through, and *respiration* is breathing—taking in oxygen to power bodily functions.

22. B: Caterpillars are the juvenile form of the butterfly. They can only reproduce once they are in their adult form.

23. C: Caterpillars eat plants, whereas butterflies feed mostly on nectar; also, butterflies need to find each other and reproduce, and caterpillars do not. Because they have different requirements and different lifestyles, they have different forms to help them best carry out those lifestyles. As for the other choices, choice A is incorrect not only because it isn't true that all insects have very different adult forms (cockroaches, for instance, look much the same throughout their lives), but also because even if it were true, the statement "it's in their genetics" wouldn't really explain anything. Choice B is incorrect because such dramatic differences in form aren't necessary in order to tell whether an animal is mature—many other animals get by without such different adult forms. Choice D is incorrect because the wings of the butterfly aren't growing all the time it's a caterpillar; they grow during the brief time the caterpillar is in a chrysalis.

24. B: Tsunamis are caused by earthquakes, but they do not cause earthquakes, nor do they cause volcanic eruptions nor wind. The sheer mass of water in the tsunami, however, can cause flooding that can do damage even beyond that done by the initial force of the water hitting the shore. The draining of the water back off into the ocean can be particularly destructive.

25. D: Although it may be difficult to prevent a tsunami from causing extensive damage, warning systems may allow people to get out of endangered areas before the tsunami hits. Strong shutters over windows can help against hurricanes and other windstorms, but they will offer little protection against tsunamis, nor is there any reason that brick buildings would withstand tsunamis better than buildings constructed of other materials. Building houses next to the shore would actually put them in *greater* danger from tsunamis because that's where tsunamis do the most damage.

26. C: The main cause of tsunamis is underwater earthquakes, although they may also be caused by underwater landslides and volcanic eruptions. Although they are sometimes informally called "tidal waves," tsunamis have nothing to do with the tides, nor do they have any connection to windstorms or to solar eclipses.

27. C: The engine of a car converts the stored energy in gasoline into motion energy (specifically, the energy of parts of the engine called pistons). Although other parts of the car do produce light (such as the headlights), sound (such as the horn and the radio), and electricity, these are not produced by the engine directly.

28. B: Heat is a form of energy. Cold is just the absence of heat. Although it could be said that speed is *related* to energy—the faster something is moving, the more energy it has—this doesn't mean speed is a *form* of energy. The same is true of weight.

29. D: Whereas the eye provides our sense of vision, the ear provides hearing, and the nose senses smell, the stomach does not help us sense the outside world; it has a different function of helping to digest our food. (Note that although the other organs are associated with the senses, those aren't necessarily their *only* functions; the ear also helps in balance, for instance, and the nose helps in breathing.)

30. A: Because animals require light to see, in dark caves, there would be nothing to see and eyes would be useless. Useless organs tend to be lost over time, as animals evolve to live without them and use the energy they would use to develop those organs for other things. Animals in caves do not necessarily suffer from significantly more inbreeding or radiation damage than animals that live elsewhere, and there's no reason why the number of eyes of different species should "average out" to any particular number. (Besides, there is at least one species of eyeless spider.)

31. B: Our sense of touch is felt in our skin. This is why we have this sense all over our bodies; if the sense of touch were in our tongues, for instance, then we would be able to feel things touching our tongues but not things touching our hands or our faces.

32. A: The eyes detect light that enters them, and then they send a signal to the brain, which processes the information from the eyes to form images and let us understand what it is we're seeing. The human skin does not have any ability to detect light, and the lungs and spleen likewise play no role in vision.

33. A: *Memory* is an organism's capacity to retain some record of past events that it can learn from and use to guide future behavior. *Hormones* are chemicals that serve various purposes in the body but are not necessarily related to memory, and although evolution is a process by which groups of organisms change over time, it has nothing to do with the learning processes of individual organisms. (As for *umami*, that's the recently discovered, fifth "basic taste" detectable by the tongue [in addition to sweet, sour, salty, and bitter], sometimes described as "meaty" and found in foods including tomatoes, shellfish, cheese, and green tea.)

34. D: *Renewable* energy sources are energy sources that aren't used up when they're used, as opposed to *nonrenewable* sources that are in limited supply and can run out. Sunlight is a renewable energy source; if we take energy from sunlight, that doesn't mean there's going to be less energy coming from the Sun in the future. (The Sun will eventually run out of energy, but that's billions of years in the future, and it's not affected by our use of its energy now; if we use solar energy, that doesn't mean the Sun is going to run out faster.) Coal, oil, and nuclear energy (which rely on certain radioactive minerals) are all nonrenewable energy sources; they exist in limited supply, and although new coal and soil may slowly form, they won't form fast enough to replenish what's been used.

Social Studies

1. D: The first 10 amendments to the US Constitution are called the Bill of Rights. The Preamble is the opening statement of the US Constitution, a kind of introduction. The Articles of Confederation predate the US Constitution as an earlier document that proved ineffective in creating a unified nation. The Declaratory Act also predates the US Constitution and was one of the British pieces of legislation that fueled colonist objection.

2. A: A delta is a body of land that forms at the mouth of a river. A strait is a narrow body of water that sits between two landforms. An estuary is a body of brackish water near a coastline. There is

water flowing into it, as from a river, and water flowing out, as to an ocean. A tongue is neither a body of land nor a body of water.

3. B: The 22nd Amendment created a term limit for the president of the United States, and no president now may serve more than two consecutive terms. Answer choice A is too low, and answer choices C and D are too high.

4. B: It was during Thomas Jefferson's administration, and at his request, that Lewis and Clark explored the Louisiana Territory. John Adams was president before Jefferson, while James Monroe and William McKinley followed him (in the latter case by about 100 years).

5. B: A type of economic system in which private businesses conduct private transactions through the exchange of goods and services is known as a market economy. The terms *social economy, sales economy,* and *circular economy* do not reflect recognized types of economic systems.

6. D: A democracy is a type of government in which all citizens have an equal voice in choosing leaders and making laws. A monarchy is a type of government with a king or queen at its head. An oligarchy is a type of government in which the power is centralized among a few people. A plutocracy is a type of government in which the wealthiest citizens have the most power and therefore make all of the governmental decisions.

7. A: The Atlantic Ocean sits on the East Coast of the United States. The Antarctic Ocean sits to the south of South America. The Indian Ocean sits to the south of the Indian subcontinent and to the east of Africa. The Pacific Ocean sits on the West Coast of the United States.

8. C: It was Sacagawea who accompanied Lewis and Clark on their journey through the Louisiana Purchase. Shoshone refers to the tribe that Sacagawea came from. Pocahontas lived during the time of the Jamestown settlement and died long before Lewis and Clark's exploration. Tecumseh was a male Shawnee who fought against the United States during the War of 1812.

9. A: By organizing and categorizing his spending to ensure he has enough money to pay bills, Jamison is making a budget. There is nothing to indicate that he has opened any type of account, so answer choice B is incorrect. Jamison appears to be making every effort to stay out of debt, so answer choice C is incorrect. Finally, the question says nothing about Jamison starting a business, so answer choice D is incorrect.

10. D: A capital resource is a resource that is used to produce something else; the electric drill is used in the construction of the house, so answer choice M is correct. The endangered fish in the estuary are a natural resource. The skilled workers in the plant are a kind of human resource. The river connected to the hydroelectric dam is also a natural resource. (The hydroelectric dam is arguably a capital resource, but the river itself remains a natural resource.)

11. B: Only answer choice B reflects the purchase of a service: The salon is providing the service of the haircut. The shoes, the newspaper, and the coffee and muffin all indicate goods that Lana purchased.

12. C: Abraham Lincoln delivered the Gettysburg Address after the deadly Battle of Gettysburg. William Howard Taft and Franklin Delano Roosevelt were president long after Gettysburg. John Adams preceded Gettysburg by more than half a century.

13. C: Scarcity—the scarcity of resources, workers, funding, and so forth—plays a major part of determining how businesses operate, what their costs will be, and where they have to make

compromises. Productivity simply describes how productive businesses are based on scarcity. Benchmarks represent goals for businesses, and they may play a role in determining how businesses operate, but they have less to do with business costs and compromises. Trading is an exchange of one resource for another and would only be reflected in the possible compromises that businesses have to make.

14. A: The star indicates the capital city, which in this case is Raleigh. Greenville, Charlotte, and Winston-Salem, while all important cities in their own right, are not the capital.

15. B: Just north of the North Carolina border is the listing of the mountains that run through the state: the Appalachian Mountains. Nearby, there is also the listing for the Great Smoky Mountains National Park, but this is (1) specifically a national park and (2) not a separate mountain range. (The Great Smoky Mountains are simply one part of the Appalachian Mountains.) More to the point, however, the only mountains that are both listed on the map as being in North Carolina and listed among the answer choices are the Appalachians. There are no Carolina or Greensboro Mountains, and the Rocky Mountains are far to the west.

16. D: Traveling from Kitty Hawk, on the east coast of the state, to Asheville, on the west side, requires going west. You would not go north, south, or east to get to Asheville from Kitty Hawk.

17. A: A cape, as noted, as a high point of land that juts into a body of water and drops off quickly. This means that a cape would need to be located near a large body of water. Only two capes are listed fitting this description: Cape Fear and Cape Hatteras. There is also an inland listing for Cape Fear, but this refers to the area near Cape Fear on the ocean and not to another cape by that name in the state.

18. B: The similar businesses that the entrepreneur will have to consider to make her own business stand out are known as competitors. Economists are people who study the economy. Producers and manufacturers are types of business owners who either produce or manufacture a product. They might very well be competitors for the entrepreneur, but these terms in themselves do not fit the meaning of *competitors*.

19. C: The Loyalists stood by the British during the Revolutionary War. The Patriots sided with the American cause. (And, many of the Patriots were militiamen, or types of soldiers.) There were no *defenders*, by this term, during the American Revolution.

20. A: The shot heard round the world occurred just before the Battles of Lexington and Concord. The Battle of Fort Washington, the Battle of Trenton, and the Battle of Saratoga all occurred later in the Revolutionary War.

21. D: The vice president is part of the executive branch of the government. The vice president serves in the legislative branch, as president of the Senate, but the vice president does not officially fall within that branch. The vice president is not part of the judicial branch, and there is no federal branch of government.

22. A: The term *bicameral* indicates that there are two houses of Congress. The other answer choices indicate too many houses.

23. B: James Madison, later the fourth president of the United States, is credited with writing the US Constitution. George Washington, the first president of the United States, did not write any of the founding documents. John Tyler (the 10th president) and Dwight D. Eisenhower (the 34th

president) were both president much later than the founding era and played no role in the founding documents.

24. D: The legend of the map explains the symbols used on the map. The scale of the map indicates how distance is adjusted for the map. The compass of the map indicates direction. The term *scheme* is not used to indicate any specific part of the map.

25. A: The term *suffrage* refers to a citizen's right to vote. This term has nothing to do with shopping, meeting, or praying.

26. B: Aylmer is faced with an opportunity cost. That is to say, by making the choice to pursue one activity—either studying or partying—Aylmer has to give up something else. Should Aylmer choose to attend the pizza party, he will lose valuable time studying. Should Aylmer choose to study, however, he will lose the chance to relax and enjoy time with his friends. The other answer choices are incorrect. Aylmer does not necessarily have a scarcity of resources, with the exception of the time that is available to him. But the term *scarcity of resources* does not refer to making a choice, as the question asks. The term *division of labor* refers to how a project is divided up according to the skills of workers, to ensure that the project is completed efficiently. It has nothing to do with the choice that Aylmer must make. Finally, Aylmer's choice, while ultimately an investment of his time, is not necessarily considered an investment opportunity.

27. A: On a map, the imaginary lines that run from east to west (but indicate location north to south) are called lines of latitude. Lines of longitude run from north to south (but indicate location east to west). The term *meridian* is simply a different word for the lines of longitude. There are no lines of standard.

28. C: Lake Huron is the fifth Great Lake. There is no Lake Ohio or Lake Niagara. Lake Minnewanka is located in the western part of Canada and is unrelated to the Great Lakes.

29. B: The Supreme Court is part of the judicial branch of government but not the legislative branch or the executive branch. There is no federal branch of government.

30. C: Nine justices sit on the Supreme Court. The other answer choices are either too low or too high.

31. D: The equator is the imaginary line that divides the Northern Hemisphere from the Southern Hemisphere. The prime meridian divides the Eastern Hemisphere from the Western Hemisphere. The Tropic of Cancer is the northernmost point at which the sun may sit directly overhead, while the Tropic of Capricorn is the southernmost point at which the sun may sit directly overhead.

32. A: Prior to the American Revolution, the Americans fought alongside the British in the French and Indian War. The Thirty Years' War was a religious war that occurred in Europe more than a century before the American Revolution. The Civil War occurred nearly a century after the American Revolution and was fought only among Americans. The Wars of the Three Kingdoms were a series of conflicts among the British, Irish, and Scottish that occurred more than a century before the American Revolution and did not include the Americans at all.

33. C: The Earth is 72 percent water, which means that the earth is approximately 70 percent water. The other answer choices are either too low or too high.

34. A: Shays' Rebellion was a result of a financial depression, following the American Revolution that left many new Americans struggling to pay debts. The Northwest Indian War, which also

followed the American Revolution, was a conflict between Americans and Native American tribes in the Northwest Territory. The Whiskey Rebellion, another post-Revolution conflict, resulted from a protest against taxation in the new nation. The War of 1812 was a conflict between Americans and the British about issues that lingered from the American Revolution.

Vocabulary

1. C: large room for public meetings

2. B: recommend

3. A: lucky

4. B: enjoyment

5. B: thin

6. A: not very often

7. C: grown up

8. C: sympathy

9. D: look up to

10. A: excellent

11. B: achieve

12. C: going up and down

13. B: desire to learn

14. A: educational talk

15. C: student

16. A: farming

17. B: number of people in an area

18. C: identify or remember

19. D: help

20. A: huge

21. D: together

22. A: number

23. B: argument

24. C: very bad

25. D: answer

26. B: false

27. C: importance

28. A: feelings

29. D: extreme

30. B: put up with

31. A: part of a city, state, or country

32. C: previous

33. C: forward movement

34. C: make smaller

Spelling

1. stomak – this should be stomach

2. chaptar – this should be chapter

3. *toona* – this should be *tuna*

4. throo – this should be through

5. *voyce* – this should be *voice*

6. mezzure – this should be measure

7. *ture* – this should be *tour*

8. *gest* – this should be *guest*

9. *brite* – this should be *bright*

10. NO MISTAKES

11. *lazzy* – this should be *lazy*

12. *vizit* – this should be *visit*

13. *beggur* – this should be *beggar*

14. *dere* – this should be *dear* or *deer*

15. *shokk* – this should be *shock*

16. *ansure* – this should be *answer*

17. *tipe* – this should be *type*

18. *pritty* – this should be *pretty*

19. *roste* – this should be *roast*

20. NO MISTAKES

21. NO MISTAKES

22. *unhapy* – this should be *unhappy*

23. *bilt* – this should be *built*

24. *serch* – this should be *search*

25. *leson* – this should be *lesson*

26. *bizzy* – this should be *busy*

27. *pruve* – this should be *prove*

Capitalization

1. A: My mom said uncle Bob

Should be: *My mom said Uncle Bob*

2. C: that's easy for you to say!

Should be: *That's Easy for You to Say!*

3. C: - december 25th

Should be: *- December 25th*

4. B: in Kansas city, Missouri

Should be: *in Kansas City, Missouri*

5. C: with doctor Jones

Should be: *with Doctor Jones*

6. A: "watch the ball, Frank!"

Should be: *"Watch the ball, Frank!"*

7. B: from the Newspaper

Should be: *from the newspaper*

8. B: Yellowstone National park

Should be: *Yellowstone National Park*

9. D: NO MISTAKES

10. C: of the koran

Should be: *of the Koran*

11. B: the Founder of

Should be: *the founder of*

12. B: world war II

Should be: *World War II*

13. B: and New year's Day are

Should be: *and New Year's Day are*

14. A: Next sunday

Should be: *Next Sunday*

15. C: without italian dressing.

Should be: *without Italian dressing.*

16. B: in the History of Italy

Should be: *in the history of Italy*

17. B: the museum of science and industry

Should be: *the Museum of Science and Industry*

18. C: said Mrs. Van buren

Should be: *said Mrs. Van Buren*

19. A: My german shepherd's name

Should be: *my German Shepherd's name*

20. D: NO MISTAKES

21. C: of king George III

Should be: of *King George III*

22. B: jupiter and saturn are

Should be: *Jupiter and Saturn are*

Punctuation

1. A: Exasperated we finally found

Should be: Exasperated, we finally found

2. A: The big game the one I've been

Should be: The big game – the one I've been

3. B: Rico bent his knees, swung for the fences

Should be: Rico bent his knees, swung for the fences,

4. B: teacher Mr. Ronson

Should be: teacher, Mr. Ronson,

5. B: the park or we can

Should be: the park, or we can

6. B: lost it's final game

Should be: lost its final game

7. A: James was disappointed

Should be: James was disappointed;

8. B: an A on the exam,

Should be: an A on the exam:

9. A: While getting ready

Should be: While getting ready,

10. A: Sam Wilma and Pedro

Should be: Sam, Wilma, and Pedro

11. B: the library Billy wants to

Should be: the library. Billy wants to

12. A: It's half past five

Should be: It's half past five;

13. A: Susie, Mom said,

Should be: "Susie, " Mom said,

14. A: Yes Mom I have

Should be: Yes, Mom, I have

15. B: a field trip we have to

Should be: a field trip, we have to

16. C: 730 tomorrow morning.

Should be: 7:30 tomorrow morning

17. B: classroom Tammy's classroom

Should be: classroom; Tammy's classroom

18. B: player Babe Ruth played

Should be: player, Babe Ruth, played

19. B: I don't think so when we asked

Should be: "I don't think so" when we asked

20. C: whats really important.

Should be: what's really important.

21. A: Yes, kids, its true that

Should be: "Yes, kids, it's true that

22. C: Bureau of Investigation FBI.

Should be: Bureau of Investigation (FBI).

How to Overcome Test Anxiety

Just the thought of taking a test is enough to make most people a little nervous. A test is an important event that can have a long-term impact on your future, so it's important to take it seriously and it's natural to feel anxious about performing well. But just because anxiety is normal, that doesn't mean that it's helpful in test taking, or that you should simply accept it as part of your life. Anxiety can have a variety of effects. These effects can be mild, like making you feel slightly nervous, or severe, like blocking your ability to focus or remember even a simple detail.

If you experience test anxiety—whether severe or mild—it's important to know how to beat it. To discover this, first you need to understand what causes test anxiety.

Causes of Test Anxiety

While we often think of anxiety as an uncontrollable emotional state, it can actually be caused by simple, practical things. One of the most common causes of test anxiety is that a person does not feel adequately prepared for their test. This feeling can be the result of many different issues such as poor study habits or lack of organization, but the most common culprit is time management. Starting to study too late, failing to organize your study time to cover all of the material, or being distracted while you study will mean that you're not well prepared for the test. This may lead to cramming the night before, which will cause you to be physically and mentally exhausted for the test. Poor time management also contributes to feelings of stress, fear, and hopelessness as you realize you are not well prepared but don't know what to do about it.

Other times, test anxiety is not related to your preparation for the test but comes from unresolved fear. This may be a past failure on a test, or poor performance on tests in general. It may come from comparing yourself to others who seem to be performing better or from the stress of living up to expectations. Anxiety may be driven by fears of the future—how failure on this test would affect your educational and career goals. These fears are often completely irrational, but they can still negatively impact your test performance.

Elements of Test Anxiety

As mentioned earlier, test anxiety is considered to be an emotional state, but it has physical and mental components as well. Sometimes you may not even realize that you are suffering from test anxiety until you notice the physical symptoms. These can include trembling hands, rapid heartbeat, sweating, nausea, and tense muscles. Extreme anxiety may lead to fainting or vomiting. Obviously, any of these symptoms can have a negative impact on testing. It is important to recognize them as soon as they begin to occur so that you can address the problem before it damages your performance.

The mental components of test anxiety include trouble focusing and inability to remember learned information. During a test, your mind is on high alert, which can help you recall information and stay focused for an extended period of time. However, anxiety interferes with your mind's natural processes, causing you to blank out, even on the questions you know well. The strain of testing during anxiety makes it difficult to stay focused, especially on a test that may take several hours. Extreme anxiety can take a huge mental toll, making it difficult not only to recall test information but even to understand the test questions or pull your thoughts together.

Effects of Test Anxiety

Test anxiety is like a disease—if left untreated, it will get progressively worse. Anxiety leads to poor performance, and this reinforces the feelings of fear and failure, which in turn lead to poor performances on subsequent tests. It can grow from a mild nervousness to a crippling condition. If allowed to progress, test anxiety can have a big impact on your schooling, and consequently on your future.

Test anxiety can spread to other parts of your life. Anxiety on tests can become anxiety in any stressful situation, and blanking on a test can turn into panicking in a job situation. But fortunately, you don't have to let anxiety rule your testing and determine your grades. There are a number of relatively simple steps you can take to move past anxiety and function normally on a test and in the rest of life.

Physical Steps for Beating Test Anxiety

While test anxiety is a serious problem, the good news is that it can be overcome. It doesn't have to control your ability to think and remember information. While it may take time, you can begin taking steps today to beat anxiety.

Just as your first hint that you may be struggling with anxiety comes from the physical symptoms, the first step to treating it is also physical. Rest is crucial for having a clear, strong mind. If you are tired, it is much easier to give in to anxiety. But if you establish good sleep habits, your body and mind will be ready to perform optimally, without the strain of exhaustion. Additionally, sleeping well helps you to retain information better, so you're more likely to recall the answers when you see the test questions.

Getting good sleep means more than going to bed on time. It's important to allow your brain time to relax. Take study breaks from time to time so it doesn't get overworked, and don't study right before bed. Take time to rest your mind before trying to rest your body, or you may find it difficult to fall asleep.

Along with sleep, other aspects of physical health are important in preparing for a test. Good nutrition is vital for good brain function. Sugary foods and drinks may give a burst of energy but this burst is followed by a crash, both physically and emotionally. Instead, fuel your body with protein and vitamin-rich foods.

Also, drink plenty of water. Dehydration can lead to headaches and exhaustion, especially if your brain is already under stress from the rigors of the test. Particularly if your test is a long one, drink water during the breaks. And if possible, take an energy-boosting snack to eat between sections.

Along with sleep and diet, a third important part of physical health is exercise. Maintaining a steady workout schedule is helpful, but even taking 5-minute study breaks to walk can help get your blood pumping faster and clear your head. Exercise also releases endorphins, which contribute to a positive feeling and can help combat test anxiety.

When you nurture your physical health, you are also contributing to your mental health. If your body is healthy, your mind is much more likely to be healthy as well. So take time to rest, nourish your body with healthy food and water, and get moving as much as possible. Taking these physical steps will make you stronger and more able to take the mental steps necessary to overcome test anxiety.

Mental Steps for Beating Test Anxiety

Working on the mental side of test anxiety can be more challenging, but as with the physical side, there are clear steps you can take to overcome it. As mentioned earlier, test anxiety often stems from lack of preparation, so the obvious solution is to prepare for the test. Effective studying may be the most important weapon you have for beating test anxiety, but you can and should employ several other mental tools to combat fear.

First, boost your confidence by reminding yourself of past success—tests or projects that you aced. If you're putting as much effort into preparing for this test as you did for those, there's no reason you should expect to fail here. Work hard to prepare; then trust your preparation.

Second, surround yourself with encouraging people. It can be helpful to find a study group, but be sure that the people you're around will encourage a positive attitude. If you spend time with others who are anxious or cynical, this will only contribute to your own anxiety. Look for others who are motivated to study hard from a desire to succeed, not from a fear of failure.

Third, reward yourself. A test is physically and mentally tiring, even without anxiety, and it can be helpful to have something to look forward to. Plan an activity following the test, regardless of the outcome, such as going to a movie or getting ice cream.

When you are taking the test, if you find yourself beginning to feel anxious, remind yourself that you know the material. Visualize successfully completing the test. Then take a few deep, relaxing breaths and return to it. Work through the questions carefully but with confidence, knowing that you are capable of succeeding.

Developing a healthy mental approach to test taking will also aid in other areas of life. Test anxiety affects more than just the actual test—it can be damaging to your mental health and even contribute to depression. It's important to beat test anxiety before it becomes a problem for more than testing.

Study Strategy

Being prepared for the test is necessary to combat anxiety, but what does being prepared look like? You may study for hours on end and still not feel prepared. What you need is a strategy for test prep. The next few pages outline our recommended steps to help you plan out and conquer the challenge of preparation.

STEP 1: SCOPE OUT THE TEST

Learn everything you can about the format (multiple choice, essay, etc.) and what will be on the test. Gather any study materials, course outlines, or sample exams that may be available. Not only will this help you to prepare, but knowing what to expect can help to alleviate test anxiety.

STEP 2: MAP OUT THE MATERIAL

Look through the textbook or study guide and make note of how many chapters or sections it has. Then divide these over the time you have. For example, if a book has 15 chapters and you have five days to study, you need to cover three chapters each day. Even better, if you have the time, leave an extra day at the end for overall review after you have gone through the material in depth.

If time is limited, you may need to prioritize the material. Look through it and make note of which sections you think you already have a good grasp on, and which need review. While you are studying, skim quickly through the familiar sections and take more time on the challenging parts.

Write out your plan so you don't get lost as you go. Having a written plan also helps you feel more in control of the study, so anxiety is less likely to arise from feeling overwhelmed at the amount to cover.

STEP 3: GATHER YOUR TOOLS

Decide what study method works best for you. Do you prefer to highlight in the book as you study and then go back over the highlighted portions? Or do you type out notes of the important information? Or is it helpful to make flashcards that you can carry with you? Assemble the pens, index cards, highlighters, post-it notes, and any other materials you may need so you won't be distracted by getting up to find things while you study.

If you're having a hard time retaining the information or organizing your notes, experiment with different methods. For example, try color-coding by subject with colored pens, highlighters, or post-it notes. If you learn better by hearing, try recording yourself reading your notes so you can listen while in the car, working out, or simply sitting at your desk. Ask a friend to quiz you from your flashcards, or try teaching someone the material to solidify it in your mind.

STEP 4: CREATE YOUR ENVIRONMENT

It's important to avoid distractions while you study. This includes both the obvious distractions like visitors and the subtle distractions like an uncomfortable chair (or a too-comfortable couch that makes you want to fall asleep). Set up the best study environment possible: good lighting and a comfortable work area. If background music helps you focus, you may want to turn it on, but otherwise keep the room quiet. If you are using a computer to take notes, be sure you don't have any other windows open, especially applications like social media, games, or anything else that could distract you. Silence your phone and turn off notifications. Be sure to keep water close by so you stay hydrated while you study (but avoid unhealthy drinks and snacks).

Also, take into account the best time of day to study. Are you freshest first thing in the morning? Try to set aside some time then to work through the material. Is your mind clearer in the afternoon or evening? Schedule your study session then. Another method is to study at the same time of day that you will take the test, so that your brain gets used to working on the material at that time and will be ready to focus at test time.

STEP 5: STUDY!

Once you have done all the study preparation, it's time to settle into the actual studying. Sit down, take a few moments to settle your mind so you can focus, and begin to follow your study plan. Don't give in to distractions or let yourself procrastinate. This is your time to prepare so you'll be ready to fearlessly approach the test. Make the most of the time and stay focused.

Of course, you don't want to burn out. If you study too long you may find that you're not retaining the information very well. Take regular study breaks. For example, taking five minutes out of every hour to walk briskly, breathing deeply and swinging your arms, can help your mind stay fresh.

As you get to the end of each chapter or section, it's a good idea to do a quick review. Remind yourself of what you learned and work on any difficult parts. When you feel that you've mastered the material, move on to the next part. At the end of your study session, briefly skim through your notes again.

But while review is helpful, cramming last minute is NOT. If at all possible, work ahead so that you won't need to fit all your study into the last day. Cramming overloads your brain with more information than it can process and retain, and your tired mind may struggle to recall even previously learned information when it is overwhelmed with last-minute study. Also, the urgent nature of cramming and the stress placed on your brain contribute to anxiety. You'll be more likely to go to the test feeling unprepared and having trouble thinking clearly.

So don't cram, and don't stay up late before the test, even just to review your notes at a leisurely pace. Your brain needs rest more than it needs to go over the information again. In fact, plan to finish your studies by noon or early afternoon the day before the test. Give your brain the rest of the day to relax or focus on other things, and get a good night's sleep. Then you will be fresh for the test and better able to recall what you've studied.

STEP 6: TAKE A PRACTICE TEST

Many courses offer sample tests, either online or in the study materials. This is an excellent resource to check whether you have mastered the material, as well as to prepare for the test format and environment.

Check the test format ahead of time: the number of questions, the type (multiple choice, free response, etc.), and the time limit. Then create a plan for working through them. For example, if you have 30 minutes to take a 60-question test, your limit is 30 seconds per question. Spend less time on the questions you know well so that you can take more time on the difficult ones.

If you have time to take several practice tests, take the first one open book, with no time limit. Work through the questions at your own pace and make sure you fully understand them. Gradually work up to taking a test under test conditions: sit at a desk with all study materials put away and set a timer. Pace yourself to make sure you finish the test with time to spare and go back to check your answers if you have time.

After each test, check your answers. On the questions you missed, be sure you understand why you missed them. Did you misread the question (tests can use tricky wording)? Did you forget the information? Or was it something you hadn't learned? Go back and study any shaky areas that the practice tests reveal.

Taking these tests not only helps with your grade, but also aids in combating test anxiety. If you're already used to the test conditions, you're less likely to worry about it, and working through tests until you're scoring well gives you a confidence boost. Go through the practice tests until you feel comfortable, and then you can go into the test knowing that you're ready for it.

Test Tips

On test day, you should be confident, knowing that you've prepared well and are ready to answer the questions. But aside from preparation, there are several test day strategies you can employ to maximize your performance.

First, as stated before, get a good night's sleep the night before the test (and for several nights before that, if possible). Go into the test with a fresh, alert mind rather than staying up late to study.

Try not to change too much about your normal routine on the day of the test. It's important to eat a nutritious breakfast, but if you normally don't eat breakfast at all, consider eating just a protein bar. If you're a coffee drinker, go ahead and have your normal coffee. Just make sure you time it so that the caffeine doesn't wear off right in the middle of your test. Avoid sugary beverages, and drink enough water to stay hydrated but not so much that you need a restroom break 10 minutes into the test. If your test isn't first thing in the morning, consider going for a walk or doing a light workout before the test to get your blood flowing.

Allow yourself enough time to get ready, and leave for the test with plenty of time to spare so you won't have the anxiety of scrambling to arrive in time. Another reason to be early is to select a good seat. It's helpful to sit away from doors and windows, which can be distracting. Find a good seat, get out your supplies, and settle your mind before the test begins.

When the test begins, start by going over the instructions carefully, even if you already know what to expect. Make sure you avoid any careless mistakes by following the directions.

Then begin working through the questions, pacing yourself as you've practiced. If you're not sure on an answer, don't spend too much time on it, and don't let it shake your confidence. Either skip it and come back later, or eliminate as many wrong answers as possible and guess among the remaining ones. Don't dwell on these questions as you continue—put them out of your mind and focus on what lies ahead.

Be sure to read all of the answer choices, even if you're sure the first one is the right answer. Sometimes you'll find a better one if you keep reading. But don't second-guess yourself if you do immediately know the answer. Your gut instinct is usually right. Don't let test anxiety rob you of the information you know.

If you have time at the end of the test (and if the test format allows), go back and review your answers. Be cautious about changing any, since your first instinct tends to be correct, but make sure you didn't misread any of the questions or accidentally mark the wrong answer choice. Look over any you skipped and make an educated guess.

At the end, leave the test feeling confident. You've done your best, so don't waste time worrying about your performance or wishing you could change anything. Instead, celebrate the successful completion of this test. And finally, use this test to learn how to deal with anxiety even better next time.

> **Review Video: Test Anxiety**
> Visit mometrix.com/academy and enter code: 100340

Important Qualification

Not all anxiety is created equal. If your test anxiety is causing major issues in your life beyond the classroom or testing center, or if you are experiencing troubling physical symptoms related to your anxiety, it may be a sign of a serious physiological or psychological condition. If this sounds like your situation, we strongly encourage you to seek professional help.

Additional Bonus Material

Due to our efforts to try to keep this book to a manageable length, we've created a link that will give you access to all of your additional bonus material:

mometrix.com/bonus948/itbsl10g4